W9-BWO-428

LOCKED IN

LOCKED IN

*The Will to Survive and
the Resolve to Live*

VICTORIA ARLEN

HOWARD BOOKS
New York   London   Toronto   Sydney   New Delhi

Howard Books
An Imprint of Simon & Schuster, Inc.
1230 Avenue of the Americas
New York, NY 10020

First Howard Books hardcover edition August 2018

HOWARD and colophon are trademarks of Simon & Schuster, Inc.

For information about special discounts for bulk purchases, please contact Simon
& Schuster Special Sales at 1-866-506-1949 or business@simonandschuster.com.

The Simon & Schuster Speakers Bureau can bring authors to your live event. For
more information or to book an event, contact the Simon & Schuster Speakers
Bureau at 1-866-248-3049 or visit our website at www.simonspeakers.com.

Interior design by Bryden Spevak

Manufactured in the United States of America

10   9   8   7   6   5   4   3   2   1

Library of Congress Cataloging-in-Publication Data is available.

ISBN 978-1-5011-7462-9
ISBN 978-1-5011-7464-3 (ebook)

For my mummy,

You truly are the wind beneath my wings.
Despite insurmountable odds and devastation,
your support, love, and faith in me and God never wavered.
You are my hero, always have been and always will be.
It's been quite the journey and it's only just the beginning.
I love you more than you will ever know.
Thank you for never giving up on me.

CONTENTS

CONTENTS

———

CONTENTS

"Father, forgive them, for they know not what they do."

—LUKE 23:34

FOREWORD

BY VALENTIN CHMERKOVSKIY

"You have a very special young woman as your partner this season," said my executive producers on *Dancing with the Stars*. "It's going to be a little different for you, and we're very excited." I was about to walk into a small ballroom dance studio in Beverly Hills to meet my Season 25 celebrity partner for the reality TV show where I'm a professional dancer. I had no idea what to expect.

As much as I love the show and everyone I work with, I also know that Hollywood doesn't always get "excited" for the same reasons I do. I nervously nodded a simple "awesome" to the producers, but in my head I was asking a million questions. "What do they mean, 'different'? Different how? What is so different about this partner that I haven't seen during the twelve seasons I've been on the show?" I would quickly find out.

I walked through the door, stepped onto the wooden parquet of the humble little ole dance studio, and caught my first sight of a beautiful young woman who stood in the center of the room. She was obviously excited with anticipation and glowing with enthusiasm.

"Hi, I'm Val," I said, starting things off as simply as I could.

"I'm Victoria," she replied.

"So tell me a little about yourself," I said. "We'll be spending quite a bit of time together in the next few months."

That was putting it mildly. On *DWTS* the celebrities and professional partners train almost daily for three months even before the show begins. My style of coaching can be quite intense, with a very challenging rehearsal regimen. Nothing about what was to come would be easy for any celebrity.

"Well, I'm a Paralympic gold medalist," she replied, with a mix of pride and humility that was really very touching.

"*Para*-lympian?!" I thought to myself, more than slightly baffled. Where was the "para"? In front of me stood a perfectly healthy, strong, vibrant girl, no different from any other twenty-three-year-old I've danced with before. What I had never seen before were Victoria's huge, extremely expressive, deep brown eyes—they were really quite exceptional.

"I don't mean to come across as rude," I said, "but why 'para'?"

The conversation that ensued and the experience I would go on to share with Victoria Arlen would change my life forever. I soon came to understand what was so special about her. It wasn't just her ability to rise above any challenge placed in front of her, including the years of paralysis that hit her beginning at age eleven, with loss of speech, loss of hearing, and finally loss of consciousness. What made Victoria special was her response to those early challenges, when someone with a less fierce sense of determination might have been tempted to give up. She never did, and neither did her strong, amazing parents.

Well, even though she still had not fully recovered feeling in her legs, Victoria had just signed on for yet another challenge, which was learning to do the Argentine tango with me. Over the course of the months we rehearsed and performed together, I discovered the source of this young woman's strength, which was quite simply her unquenchable love of life. She loved life so much that it amounted to her particular superpower. She simply refused to be defeated, no matter what obstacles were thrown in her way. Victoria's one-of-a-kind perspective on life taught me the greatest lesson anyone could ever teach someone: "Don't take a single breath for granted."

In this book, you will get to know a girl from an ordinary family who was placed in the most extraordinary circumstances imaginable. Instead of giving up, Victoria, her mother, and her father chose to fight on for dear life, literally. She is not just an American hero for her medals in the Paralympics. She's a human hero for her triumphs over something that universally unites us, our mortality and the fight for life. There's no greater example of the human spirit than that, no better demonstration of strength in family and faith. Victoria's story will inspire you with a sense of purpose, helping to ignite a passion and appreciation for life that you may never have thought possible.

I'm incredibly grateful to have been Victoria's partner on *DWTS*, thankful to her family for sharing her with me, and actually indebted to the whole wide universe for putting us together. Victoria allowed me to be a small part of her incredible story, one that will certainly leave a mark on the world. Reading her story, I think you'll come to respect, honor, and love this woman just as I did, and cherish the opportunity to get to know her.

—Valentin Chmerkovskiy

1

HOW DID I GET HERE?

January 2009

I hear commotion in the darkness. I gasp for air, but I feel like I'm drowning. A strong pressure crushes my chest, forcing my lungs to contract against my will.

Air!

I need air!

I need to breathe!

Somebody, please help me!

Machines urgently ping. Panicked voices shout all around me. Suddenly, bright light blinds me as I struggle to grab whatever is down my throat. I realize my arms are strapped down and can't move. Multiple hands hold down my convulsing body, and my bed is being quickly pushed through a white-walled hallway at an alarmingly fast speed.

"You are okay, Victoria," I hear over and over again. I'm confused. All I can think is *BREATHE!* And then, I plunge again into total darkness.

• • •

My eyes open to searing bright light, and I hear a loud, screeching noise. My body begins to shake uncontrollably, and a painful electricity surges through my body, causing it to convulse and thrash about. I see strangers running into the room, yelling. Their voices sound scared; their hands push me down.

As the seizure subsides, I try to get my bearings.

Where am I?

Brightly colored balloons are tied to my bed, and several stuffed animals are around the room. My vision is blurry, but as I focus my eyes, I see cheery cards and posters on the wall, saying, "We love you. Get well. We miss you. Stay strong."

Why would anyone say they miss me?

Where have I been?

Get well?

Stay strong?

What's wrong with me?

I feel fine.

I don't get it.

Where am I?

What is going on?

Am I in the hospital?

Why?

How long have I been out of it?

I hear my mom in the background. Surely, she can tell me what's going on. "Mom, Mom!" I shout, but she doesn't react.

HELLO!

Why can't she hear me?!

Can anyone hear me?

I quickly realize I have no control of my body, not even my eyes. I can see, but only what's directly in front of me. When I try to sit up, I feel disconnected from my body. I can't move or make any sound.

I am literally locked inside my own body.

This can't be happening.

This can't be happening!

Help!

Somebody, please help me!

My heart races and my head spins. I try to make sense of what's going on. I have so many questions.

What year is it?

I think, 2006? But I'm not certain.

How long have I been here?

I hope not long.

What happened?

My memory is fuzzy.

Am I going to be okay?

I'm not sure.

I'm overcome with panic. I want to scream for help. I try to calm down, but that only makes things worse. I'm lost and confused. Why won't someone just please tell me what is going on.

I'm scared.

I'm really, really scared.

I can't move a single muscle. No matter how hard I try to scream for help, nothing comes out. I want to breathe and scream and speak. I have so many questions, and I have no memory of how I got here.

I gotta get outta here!

Help!

Somebody, help!

Claustrophobia creeps in, and my panic escalates. I have to find something—anything—to keep my brain sane and ease the panic that's overtaking me.

Think, Victoria.

Wait . . .

You can think—

clear as day.

My body refuses to function, but my brain is somehow operating normally. Completely normally.

How can this be?

My brain.

My memories.

My knowledge. It's all here.

You're still here, Victoria.

You're still you.

My mind is the only reassurance and calm I have. It is the only thing I can control. And then it dawns on me that my ability to think is the most important function of all. The thought of literally losing my mind is beyond terrifying. Thankfully, I can think and understand.

Sanity check . . .

Okay . . .

My name is Victoria Arlen.

I am the daughter of Larry and Jacqueline Arlen.

My brothers are LJ, William, and Cameron.

I enjoy swimming, dancing, and hockey.

I love my fluffy dog, Jasmine.

My favorite color is pink.

Okay, let's make it a little more challenging:

What's two plus two?

Four.

Four times four?

Sixteen.

You're good, Victoria.

Your brain is okay.

Thank you, God.

I have my mind and my memories, and as far as I know, I have my sanity. I'm still here—I remind myself of that over and over again.

But, how did I get here?

Nothing comes to mind. I remember an absolutely excruciating head pain, and I remember being rushed into an ambulance, and then everything goes dark. Now, I'm alive and can think. But I have no memory of how I got here or why I can't move or talk.

I try so hard to remember.

Think, Victoria.

Remember.

When I try to think back before the headaches and the seizures, all I can remember is being healthy. I'd always been healthy. In fact, I was probably the healthiest of the Arlen bunch (although we were a relatively healthy family). I'd always had a crazy amount of energy and would go and go and go until my mum made me go to bed. I craved adventure and always allowed my imagination to go for miles and miles. I loved running around with my brothers, and I played every sport my parents would allow. There were never enough hours in the day to do all I wanted to do. Even then, I'd wanted to change the world and make a difference.

How could I lose all of that?

How could the girl who could do everything not even be able to wiggle a finger?

I keep forcing myself to think. Since I can't work any other muscle in my body, I might as well use the one that works, my brain. I remember back to the summer before fifth grade, when I was ten. My mummy took me to the doctor with what seemed to be a bug bite in my left ear. The doctor hadn't been concerned about it, but then I started getting ear infections, which continued throughout the entire summer. The doctors diagnosed me with swimmer's ear, but that didn't make sense because I had swum for years without any problems.

I remember that I'd developed asthma in the fall. Then, I had several rounds of pneumonia alternating with what the doctor called the "flu." These episodes often included fainting spells. It seemed I'd have one or two good weeks, but then I'd come down with something.

I still did well in school and sports, but somehow, as my mummy would say, "it was as if the stars were misaligned." But no one was too awfully concerned because I always bounced back and went back to my normal routine.

But about a year later, on April 29, 2006, I do not bounce back . . .

2

IT'S ALL IN YOUR HEAD

April to July 2006

Ouch!

It feels as if a knife is piercing my right side. I try to sit up, but I'm met with excruciating pain, unlike anything I've ever felt before. I slowly get out of bed and make my way downstairs. "Mummy, something doesn't feel right."

Assuming it's another flu-like episode, my mum guides me to the couch and tucks me in. It's a Sunday. We had just gotten back from a magical Disney trip the day before. All I can think about is going back to school and seeing my friends. I am in fifth grade and almost done with my first year at middle school. The first day back to school from vacation is always fun.

But instead of going to school the next day, I end up in the emergency room, being poked and prodded and questioned. The needles scare me, and the "juice" (dye) I have to drink for the CT scan makes me vomit. My family has a history of appendicitis, and since the pain is on my right side, it seems the likely cause. After an overnight in the hospital with no reprieve from the pain, doctors decide to remove my appendix. My parents and I hope that this is the fix, so we can go home the next day and resume our happy lives.

But the pain doesn't go away, even after the surgery scars are healed. I find myself again in the emergency room, this time at a world-renowned children's hospital—"best in the world"—an hour away from our home. After a CT scan and blood work, the doctors have no definitive answer other than post-surgical pain. Unconcerned, they send me home.

It still hurts.

Two weeks pass, and the pain in my side has gotten increasingly worse. I now have regular flu-like symptoms, and I'm losing weight fast. No matter how much I eat, the weight will not stay on. I was slim to start with, but now, I'm way too skinny. The pain is so bad, I can barely function. I can't sleep, and I don't even have the energy to get off the couch. Which is unlike healthy Victoria. I was NEVER on the couch. I can't go to school or play sports or hang with my friends. I am a prisoner to this suffering, and it is slowly but surely taking over my life.

The only "relief" the doctors offer is recommendations to see other doctors, who prescribe heavy-duty pain meds and send me on my way. Pain meds don't help and the reactions to the medications only make it worse.

Along with the pain comes overwhelming weakness. Getting out of bed and down the stairs is a challenging task. I can remember the days when I ran up and down the stairs; now each step is like climbing a steep mountain. Fighting to stay upright is an all-consuming chore.

No.

No.

No.

Just when I think the pain in my side can't get worse, it begins to spread, starting in my toes and slowly working its way up my leg. My right foot has been asleep for two days. I try to walk, but it drags beside me like an anchor. My mum takes me to my primary-care doctor who has known me since birth. She explains that I am still in extreme pain even after having my appendix removed, that I've lost a lot of weight, and that now, I'm having trouble walking. The doctor just nods his head and says, "I don't know. She is a triplet. Maybe she is doing it for attention." Instead of referring me to a neurologist, he insists that I see a psychologist and "snap out of it." How could being a triplet cause this? Attention is the last thing I want. Needing "help" frustrates me beyond belief. Besides, what eleven-year-old can make all of this up?

We've all heard someone say, "It's all in your head." Most of the time, it's a lighthearted way to say, "toughen up" or "get a grip." I never thought it held any serious meaning. But the doctors I see use phrases like that or words like *psychosomatic* as fancy ways of saying, "You're doing it for attention" or "We have no idea." Basically, they don't believe me.

I start hearing things like, "The pain you think you feel doesn't really exist, Victoria. Yes, the reflex in your right leg is gone and you're having trouble walking, but don't worry, it's all in your head. Just snap out of it, and you'll be okay," or "You're not feeling well? You're a triplet. You just want attention. Nothing seems to be medically wrong. You're fine."

I'm not fine.

Can somebody help me?

Or tell me what's going on?

Please?

Please.

Something is seriously wrong—I know it—but no doctor seems to care. I am fading fast . . .

Please.

Please believe me.

Please help me.

I feel that doctor after doctor has failed me. After a visit to a prominent children's hospital in Massachusetts, it seemed that I had been labeled a "crazy person" and that no doctor would take me seriously.

But . . . I'm in pain.

So much pain.

Why won't you listen to me?

Something is seriously wrong!

I'm not crazy.

Please.

I'm not crazy.

My family and I don't know it at the time, but we've just begun a long road of misdiagnoses.

• • •

It is now June, summer is quickly approaching, and all I want is to play with my friends and finish the school year. I pray every night to be okay and get stronger. I can take the pain—I've gotten used to it—but I can't take the weakness in my legs. Without my legs, I'm quickly losing my independence. I've already missed out on so much. I just want to go back to living my life.

Both feet are beginning to burn like I am walking on hot coals. Sharp pain shoots up my legs. Every day, the pain creeps higher and higher, becoming more and more intense. The pain in my legs is the same kind of pain I feel in my right side. My right foot continues to drag, and now, my knees are buckling. Every time I stand, they give out right from under me, and I drop to the floor. I am determined not to have anyone help me, so I grab on to furniture and walls just to stay upright.

Surely this is going to pass.

Wrong.

My legs are getting weaker and weaker. I no longer can wiggle my toes. The pain continues to escalate. And then, abruptly, one morning the pain is gone. As much as I want to celebrate being pain free, I'd rather take the pain than what was left after the pain . . . nothing.

No more movement. No more function. Nothing. Deep down, I know . . .

Something is seriously wrong.

By late June, doctors in two major Massachusetts hospitals had labeled my condition as "psychological." Unable to explain what is wrong the doctors use the label "psychological" to put some sort of label to my condition. The doctors continue to write me off and refuse to believe me or help me. In a desperate attempt for answers, my mummy takes me to an alternative healer in Connecticut. The healer is incredibly concerned and quickly makes a phone call. Before we know it, we are on our way to yet another major hospital, this time in New York City. At first, the doctors are genuinely concerned and run a series of tests. But as test after test comes back inconclusive, they scratch their heads. What causes a normal eleven-year-old girl to go from active and healthy . . . to this?

After about a week of tests and failed physical therapy, one of the top doctors walks in, holds her hands up, and says, "I don't know." And then, she walks out, leaving us with nothing except a prescription for more physical therapy—and a wheelchair.

Wheelchair?

This is only temporary, right?

My only experience with wheelchairs was when one of my fourth-grade friends broke his leg in a motorcycle accident. He had a really cool yellow chair, and I remember wondering what it was like for him to sit all day. I never, ever imagined that I would one day sit in a wheelchair, and that it would be the only way I'd get around for a very long time.

This is when I truly begin to comprehend that my legs are not working. I cannot fathom or process the disconnect.

Why can't I walk?

Why can't I feel my legs?

Wiggle, toe.

Wiggle, please!

All my life, I had been active. I'd run around and danced without any issues. And now? I can't even wiggle my toes. I spend hours looking at my feet, desperately searching for any sign of life. Each passing minute creates more anxiety and confusion.

HELP!

If I could just be better in time for field hockey camp in July. I am determined to be a starter in sixth grade. But you have to be able to walk to go to field hockey camp . . .

• • •

The fireworks light up the sky, and people around the lake are cheering. It is July Fourth weekend. I am sitting in my wheelchair at my family's lake house, confused and sad. I can't run around with the other kids, and I am so sick that even sitting in my wheelchair is exhausting. Just last summer, I was running around with everyone and watching the fireworks, not a worry in the world. Now, I hold on to that memory like a lifeline. My sparkle and joy are slowly slipping from my fingertips. My world is imploding . . .

What is happening to me?

Where have you gone, Victoria?

Why is nobody giving me any answers?

Why won't the doctors believe me?

Am I really crazy?

I know I'm not crazy and that what I'm feeling is real, but I feel let down by the medical world that keeps saying it is "all in my head." I am getting worse, but the "experts" don't believe me and don't help me.

My mummy is my constant source of hope. She refuses to accept that "nothing could be done." Her faith in me keeps me sane and strong. But even she can't stop what happens next.

After that July Fourth weekend, my entire body begins to shut down, bit by bit.

It's as if the "circuits" that control my bodily functions are "clicking off" one by one. Like the circuits of the house that keep all the electronic functions working—the lights, the fridge, the

TV—the switches to my internal circuit board are slowly shutting off. Function after function becomes increasingly difficult, until each one just shuts off.

I, I, I can't swallow.

The food is getting stuck, Mummy.

Eating has never been an issue for me. For as long as I can remember, I've had a never-ending appetite. Suddenly, eating is physically challenging. I try to swallow, but it feels like something is blocking my throat. Each swallow becomes harder and harder.

Cough. Food is still there.

Try again.

Cough, cough, cough.

Food is stuck.

One more time, come on, Victoria.

Cough!

Cough!

Starting to choke, help!

These episodes become more and more frequent. The muscles in my throat and mouth become weaker and weaker. Until . . .

The muscles in my throat no longer work . . . *click.*

My ability to move my legs and toes was already gone, but now the ability to use my arms and fingers is dwindling.

It's like when a baby struggles to grab something. She knows she wants the object or toy, but she can't find the coordination to get her little arm to the right place. She tries and tries until eventually, she finds her way, and movement becomes second nature.

But I am moving in the opposite direction. Simple things like grabbing a cup of water become harder and harder. I want to move my hands and fingers, but they won't cooperate. The connection is slowly disappearing—until . . .

I can no longer control my hands and fingers . . . *click*.

I'm requiring more and more help, and holding on to my independence becomes harder and harder. I exert all the energy I have to take care of myself. I fight for control and to stay the driver of this car, but it's spinning out of control and flying down the highway at speeds I can't control. It seems that each morning, I wake up to terrifying revelations that make me more dependent than ever.

I lose my independence . . . *click*.

Then, my greatest fear starts becoming a reality. I have moments when I can't recall simple things, like who I am and where I am and who my family members are. It feels like my mind is short-circuiting, going in and out.

These moments become increasingly frequent, and when they strike, my ability to speak becomes difficult. I know what I want to say, but I can't find the right word or make the connection between my brain and mouth. Then I snap out of it, and I'm fine. One minute, I know who my mummy is, and the next I don't. I keep going in and out of lucidity, and every time, I pray that I'll snap out of it.

My name is Victoria Arlen.

My name is Victoria Arlen.

My name is Victoria Arlen.

My name . . .

is . . .

?

What's my name?!

What's my name?!

No.

No.

Please, no.

Make it stop, please!

My mental stability . . . *click.*

In my rarer lucid moments, at least I have my voice. I can still communicate with my family and let them know what I'm experiencing. But then, one day . . .

Can anyone hear me?

Hello!

My voice!

My voice!

Where is my voice?!

Completely gone. I try to make words but can only produce strained, nonsensical mumbles and groans.

My ability to communicate is gone . . . *click.*

• • •

In my fifth-grade art class, we used a vise, which would crank two metal slabs together to hold our artwork in place. It looked like something out of a Viking movie. And it looked painful for the poor piece of paper.

And now, that's how I feel—like my head is being squeezed in a vise, and the pressure keeps getting stronger and stronger until it is unbearable. I lose consciousness because of the pain, and I want to throw up. No reprieve and no relief, just squeezing and constricting my brain. This headache goes on for what seemed like a century (but in fact was two days). Then *it all goes dark*.

The final switch—lights out . . . *click*.

Floating into a black hole, I am trapped in this darkened state, but I don't even realize it. I've slipped away from myself, my family, and all that I know. I am trapped in a ghost of a mind, locked inside a body that does not connect with me.

The Victoria my friends knew and my family loved is nonexistent. The lights are off and there is nothing left that works. Everything that made me, me. Gone.

Victoria Catherine Arlen, born September 26, 1994, in Boston, Massachusetts, to Larry and Jacqueline Arlen . . . *erased*.

Entering *hell*.

3

HELL

Early August 2006

After I lose my cognitive function, my parents again take me to the emergency room at a prominent children's hospital in Massachusetts, where I am immediately admitted. While in the hospital, I once again have another battery of painful tests . . . with, once again, no answers. After a few days, my parents were taken to a conference room in the hospital and told about a "pain management and rehab facility," which the doctors say could "help me." My parents are desperate to get help for me, and there is concern that if I came home, I would surely die. At the time, they feel they had little choice but to agree or risk being charged with not properly taking care of me.

The "pain management" facility is actually an older, run-down section of the children's hospital. The rooms are similar to dorm rooms, and the walls are white and bare. My parents are initially unaware that it is actually an unmarked psychiatric facility, where visitation is restricted, and clearance is required to get in.

During this time, I go in and out of cognitive awareness. But I have many memories of that time—most of which I wish more than anything that I could forget.

In Sunday school, I learned about heaven and hell. Heaven was described as a beautiful place where God lived—a place full of love and light. Hell, on the other hand, was described as a very bad place where bad people go, where there is fire and torment, and lots of very bad things happen. But I learn during my time here that there are forms of hell on this earth.

As I am wheeled into my new "living" quarters, I am disoriented and confused—but I have enough awareness to know that my parents are leaving me. They tell me over and over again that they love me and that they will see me again soon. I try to scream and cry out as my parents say good-bye, but the sound refuses to come out of my mouth.

Please don't leave me here.

Please.

After they leave, rough hands grab my shoulders, and I hear an aggressive-sounding male voice say, "Your parents are not coming back until you snap out of it. You can't fool us like you've fooled them." That is when I know that this is not a place of healing and help.

They are not going to help me.

They think I'm crazy.

Please, let me out of here.

Let me go home.

I'm not crazy.

I'm not crazy.

I'm not crazy.

I learn later that my mummy has a type of nervous breakdown on the drive home. Then after arriving home, she begins to research the place that is supposedly going to "help" her daughter. But she quickly realizes that I am not in a "pain management and rehab facility"—it is actually a *psychiatric ward*. My parents immediately begin searching for a way to get me out of there.

I'm trapped.

And they are gonna kill me.

I remember them taunting me and telling me over and over again:

"We don't believe you."

"Snap out of it!"

"Aw, your mommy isn't here to help you now, is she?"

It seems they are trying to inflict pain to "break me" to "snap me out of it."

I'm NOT pretending!

Somebody help me!

Please.

Many of the nurses and nursing assistants are rough with me, but one in particular is the worst. I remember her being in her mid-fifties, heavyset, wearing big glasses, with blond-gray hair and a bowl-style haircut. Let's call her "F."

In the mornings, "F" puts me in a cold shower and taunts me when my upper-body strength gives out and I fall. I am unable to swallow food, but because "F" believes I'm faking it, she force-feeds me. And when the food gets stuck, I cough and struggle for air. Only when I am barely able to breathe does she intervene and stop. And this happens over and over again. Needless to say, I will *never* eat a chocolate chip muffin or cherry yogurt again. The irony of which is that I have never been a fan of chocolate or cherry. She doesn't even ask what I liked or disliked. Then, because I am "choosing not to swallow my food," she and another nurse wheel me into a room where "F" aggressively shoves a nasal gastric tube up my nose and forcefully feeds me a liquid meal. Then, instead of leaving it in, she rips it out and repeats this process for every meal, three times a day. I will later learn that nasal gastric tubes can be left in, instead of being inserted and pulled out multiple times a day. When my mummy asks why they are not leaving it in, the head nurse says, "The idea is to make her eat again, and the only way we are going to do that is to make sure that the process is uncomfortable and not a pleasant experience." Of course, my mummy is livid, but she has no control.

I am often left alone, and when I need to use the bathroom, I try to get to the bathroom myself, oftentimes left to lose control of my bladder and pass out on the floor. I am frequently left on the floor for quite some time, so you can imagine the state I am in. My *dignity* is taken away from me over and over again with claims like, "You're doing this to yourself," and "It's all in your head," and "You deserve this."

I don't deserve this . . .

Nobody deserves this.

I am already in a very confused state of mind, and this mistreatment makes me feel like a criminal who has committed a horrific crime.

Please just let me go home.

I have done nothing wrong.

I've never understood why people hurt other people. Even when I was young, I'd get so upset when I saw kids being unkind to one another. I'd pray every night and ask God to make everyone love one another and help one another.

Even *if* the nurses and doctors here are convinced that their rough and cruel methods are helping me, I have to say that unkindness *never* makes things better. And even *if* my sickness were psychological, how would inflicting pain make me better? If anything, love should be the core of any kind of treatment. Whether your situation is mental or physical, there should never be abuse of any nature for treatment. Inflicting pain does not take away pain.

And one more thing: my pain is *not* all in my head.

I'm a prisoner.

In a painful prison.

Not only are my parents given limited times to visit with me, they are not allowed to stay with me overnight—and the nighttime is when the roughest treatment occurs. I've always been afraid of the dark, and this place reaffirms my fear of the night.

As the days and nights pass, I feel myself becoming weaker and less engaged. The medical staff has instilled so much fear in me that I no longer make eye contact with anyone. I keep my head hunched over. A brief glimpse of myself in the mirror reveals a gray, skeletal, defeated face. Sunken cheeks, glazed-over eyes with no trace of the sparkle that once danced there.

How can that zombie in the mirror be me?

Where is the smiley, energetic, silly girl?

Where is that sparkle?

I used to have a dimple on my left cheek, and it always showed because I always smiled. Now my face is too gaunt for me to see that dimple. I can't smile, I can't talk, and I can barely hold up my head. I don't want to see the horror on the faces of my family when they visit, and so I choose not to look into their eyes.

I am powerless.

There is no worse feeling than not being able to fight back.

Why have you left me here?

I will later learn that my family is desperately trying to get me out of the facility. They are told that they can't remove me because I need psychological help. But they instinctively know that this place will kill me if they don't rescue me soon. They work hard to assemble a team of lawyers and doctors, and they begin to come up with a plan to get me discharged. Meanwhile, I am fighting to survive.

In the midst of this living hell, one nurse is kind and caring and truly means well. She takes care of me and advocates for me, and when my parents come to visit, she lets them know that I don't belong there and that they need to get me out.

But unfortunately, this nurse isn't frequently assigned to me. Apparently, "F" has taken a "liking" to me and seems to *always* be assigned to me. When my parents visit, she tries to convince them that I am putting on a "show" and that when they aren't around, I am "perfectly fine."

My body is shutting down and slowly failing me. I barely have the energy to keep my eyes open. I'm not sure how much more I can take, but I keep trying and fighting. "F" and many of the nurses relentlessly try to get me to "snap out of it." And their tactics are not necessarily humane. I wouldn't wish what they did to me on my worst enemy.

This is it.

Give up the fight.

Just make it stop.

How much more of this can I take?

By now, I barely have the energy to keep my eyes open. I don't know how much more I can take, but something within me keeps trying.

Try. To. Fight.

Take. Back. Your. Dignity.

I, I, I, can't.

I don't want to fight anymore.

I feel desperate to live but even more desperate to leave.

In many ways it feels as if I am stuck between two worlds. What if I just quit trying? Maybe that's my way out and I can leave the struggle behind and die. Be free, finally. I cannot remember the last time I felt free. I am in excruciating pain and feel so sick that death seems welcome. Pain and suffering have become my identity and my existence. And I just pray that God will have mercy on me and take it all away.

One particular night in the facility brings me head-on with the possibility of death. As bad as things have been, something is different this night, very different. My heart is racing, and the pain is at its worse. My breathing is labored, and my body starts convulsing. I am dying. My body, curled in a fetal position, is giving in and giving up.

So this is what dying feels like.

I am alone in my room. The staff has locked the door. I try to scream for help, but I can barely breathe. I look out the window, up into the sky, and have this terrifying realization that this is the end. My body has fought all it can fight, and it is time to let go. The pain is increasing, and my breathing is decreasing. My body writhes and shakes and feels as if it is going to explode. My head spins. Everything is tense. I can't even cry. The only comfort I have is from my blankies that Mummy left with me—the ones I've had since I was a baby. The soft, familiar fabric provides a small comfort, and for just a moment I close my eyes and feel like I am home.

I wanna go home.

Please, let me go home.

I wanna go home.

Reality quickly rips me from this bliss as I look over at the doorway and my empty room, with its concrete white walls and dirty ceiling tiles, and realize the most devastating part about this: not only am I going to die in this cold and horrible place, but I am going to die alone. All alone, with nobody to comfort me or hold me. Never being able to say good-bye to my family or my friends or the life I left behind. Never being able to swim again, dance again, play hockey, go to school, drive a car, or even have a boyfriend. Never being able to live again, see the world, and smile and laugh. My left dimple forever a distant memory captured in photographs and home movies. My big brown eyes forever forgotten. I honestly can't remember the last time I smiled and laughed. The doctors will not even care and, if anything, will probably be happy to have the room open up. After all, they thought I was crazy anyway.

This is what they wanted.

They broke me.

And nobody will ever know what truly happened here.

Nobody will ever know the horrible things the doctors and nurses did to me.

The horrific things they said and did to me.

And

They'll never know how hard I fought and how much I endured.

I'll be silenced.

Forever.

And they will keep hurting other children like me.

But at this point I am so sick and in the worst pain you can imagine. All I want is for it to be over. Even if that means dying. I can't even cry, no matter how hard I try. There is literally nothing left. My body is done, and I am done.

I know that I am so close to being free, no more pain, and so close to leaving this painful world. I welcome death like an old friend. A friend I never knew I ever wanted until this moment. I yearn for freedom and a pain-free moment. Just a moment to smile and breathe without feeling as if I am being stabbed. At this point death seemed like the only good option. The world around me was far from ideal and the thought of staying and suffering any longer is unbearable. I can't take any more. I never wanted to die or give up, and I am terribly afraid—not necessarily of death itself, but of leaving everyone behind and not having the chance to live and accomplish my dreams. I'm also more afraid of living another day in this hell. If I had the strength, I probably would've already killed myself.

I'd had such big dreams since childhood. No gold medal, no

acting, no being a television host or on *Dancing with the Stars*, and no changing the world. These were dreams, among many others, that I promised myself I would achieve one day. Unfortunately, that day would never come, those dreams were stolen from me by these nurses and doctors. They are determined to break me; they win.

I'm sorry I wasn't stronger.

I'm so sorry.

As I lie there dying, I can't help but think about how my story is ending and how defeated I feel. I am a victim and there is no worse feeling. And as an athlete, there is no worse feeling than losing. I have lost the biggest battle of my life. Literally.

This is not how my story was supposed to end . . .

Dying is awful, but dying because of others' actions and mistakes is a whole different level of awful. Even at eleven, I know that this is not how my story is supposed to end. I have not even come close to living the life I had imagined. But I just know I can't fight anymore, and I have to let go. I know I have been strong, but it is truly time to hand it over to God. I just can't help but pray.

Please God, please help me.

Tell my family that I love them.

Tell them that I'm sorry.

I never wanted things to end like this.

Please watch over my mummy especially.

And let my parents know that it wasn't their fault.

The thought of leaving my family terrifies me. When you're a triplet, there's a lifelong commitment to stick together. Come into this world together and leave together (or something like that). My older brother, LJ, is my teddy bear and protector. I haven't even brought a boy home for him to interrogate. And my parents—oh, my parents. I know they could never live with themselves if I were to die here, especially alone.

I know deep down that I have not truly lived yet. I need to find everything I have to stay alive. But the will to live compared to the thought of leaving this hell behind is too much to bear. So I pray, harder than I have ever prayed.

Please God, save me from this hell I'm living in.

I don't want to die.

But I can't live any longer here.

Please, God.

Don't let me die here.

Save me.

I'm afraid to close my eyes because I don't know if they'll open again. Fear takes over my body like a ship taking on water, desperate to stay afloat but aware of its demise.

Stay awake, Victoria.

Stay alive.

Don't be afraid.

Be strong.

Fear is an all-encompassing and confusing emotion. You never know how hard it will hit you or what will cause it. Later, I will know that many factors contributed to the fear I am feeling, but deep down I am afraid of being alone, of suffering in silence and leaving without ever having a chance.

How can my story end like this?

Abused.

In pain.

Alone.

A victim of this sickness and this horrific place.

I want to live and be free, but I know that this is not a reality and, frankly, impossible at this moment. The cost of surviving any more of this hell is far too great of a debt that I cannot pay.

I cannot fight anymore.

I'm sorry.

I'm so, so, so sorry.

I struggle to find the strength to die with dignity. To not cry. To not be afraid. And to be strong and remind myself that I fought hard.

Dear Victoria:

You did so well. You've lived a good life. You figured out math and always got good grades. You swam fast, loved your family, and always lived boldly. Your smile could light up a room and it will light up in heaven as well. You fought hard. And you did NOT give up. Unfortunately, the pain and this sickness was a bigger battle than anyone could've imagined. And in this place, you were outnumbered. An army of one fighting far too many enemies with weapons far greater than yours. And I know this wasn't how you planned your life or how it would end, but it's okay. Sometimes, things do not go as planned. But do not be afraid. Although it was a short life, it was a good one. A really, really good one. A life never to be forgotten. It's time to get your wings and finally be free.

Jesus, please take me.

To God:

Thank you, God, for a beautiful life. Please surround my family with your love and mine. Let me shine over them every day like the rainbows I used to draw for as long as they will live. Let them know that I am always with them. Please hold them when they cry out to me and protect them when the grief is far too great to bear. And please, let them never forget how much I love them. And please, let my brothers live boldly and fearlessly with me as the wind beneath their wings.

To My Family:

First and foremost, thank you for the most incredible eleven years. I can't help but smile when I think of all of you and how much fun we all had. From the lake house, to the hockey rink, to skiing, dance parties, and the many fun trips and adventures, being a part of this family was by far the most incredible gift from God. I was beyond lucky to have you all in my life. And I am so sorry that things had to end like this. There truly are no words that I can begin to put together to say how much I will miss all of you and how much each of you mean to me. In fact, I honestly think that the reason I held on so long was because of all of you. I tried so hard to fight, I truly did, because I wanted more time with all of you. I'm sorry that we couldn't have more time. William, Cameron, and LJ, you boys were the best brothers a girl could ever ask for. William, I'll miss watching you play hockey and playing street hockey with you and climbing trees pretending we were monkeys. Cameron, I'll miss your hugs and how you always made me laugh and called me beautiful. I'll miss being the "three musketeers" and how we did everything together. And LJ, I'll miss the way you protected me, watched out for me, and always made me smile. You were the best role model and big brother and I will never forget all that you did for me. Boys, I hope you all live boldly and fearlessly, and I pray that my passing does not take away your joy and your smiles. I pray that you all live beautiful and incredible lives. You'll know I'm with you wherever you go. You may not see me, but know I'll be there always. I will never leave your side. And finally, Mummy and Daddy, thank you for always trying to help me and loving me so beautifully and passionately. It pains me that you're not here and I know that you are fighting for me and will never stop. Although this fight unfortunately was not how we planned, please know that I know you did EVERYTHING to help me and this was NOT your fault. I love you more than life itself and wish more than anything I could have one last snuggle with you both. I'll miss your smile, Mummy, and how you lit up a room everywhere you go. And Daddy, I'll miss your laugh and all of your silly shenanigans and you calling me Tweetie Bird. It makes me sad to know that you won't be able to walk me down the aisle when I'm grown. I'll always be your little girl. I wish more than anything I had more time, but I'll see you all very soon. This was never how I planned things nor was this how I was planning to spend my last moments. But please know that I love you all so much. And I'm so sorry that I could not hold on. Live with light and love and without fear, for me.

I'll keep watching over you, always.

I am afraid, but I am trying to find meaning and peace among the chaos and pain.

Please, just make it quick.

I can't take this anymore.

Please.

Please.

Suddenly I'm reminded of a Bible verse. "Have I not commanded you? Be strong and courageous. Do not be afraid; do not be discouraged, for the LORD your God will be with you wherever you go." Joshua 1:9 (NIV)

Please, God.

Be with me.

Make it quick.

Let me go.

Let me fly free.

I'm really scared . . . But then I remember . . .

"Fear not, for I *am* with you;

Be not dismayed, for I *am* your God.

36

I will strengthen you, Yes, I will help you,

I will uphold you with My righteous right hand."

—*Isaiah 41:10 (NKJV)*

The fear, to my surprise, quickly disappears as this incredible calmness and love surround me. I can only describe it as the love of God. He is holding me, and I know that whatever happens, it's going to be okay. At even one of the worst times of my life, God is by my side, holding me, loving me, and protecting me. Even though I'm alone in the flesh, I know I'm not alone with God by my side. I am at total peace. If I stay or if I go, I am at peace.

It's gonna be okay.

I say my thank-you prayer to God and slowly and peacefully try to close my eyes.

"Victoria?"

What?

"Victoria, wake up. It's Mummy."

Mummy?

Is it really you?

My mummy rushes into my room with two paramedics and a stretcher. "Mummy's got you; we're getting you out of here." I hear her say this over and over again.

Am I dead?

Is this a dream?

I'm bewildered and don't even have the strength to move or

motion to let her know I hear her. I'm quickly put on a stretcher and they begin to roll me out of the facility. I look around at the bare walls and the nurses and doctors standing in the hallway. And then I see her, the one who made my life a living hell—"F." I want to yell out like a little schoolgirl, "Ha, ha, you can't catch me!" Instead, I say it on the inside and picture her getting smacked by an angry dolphin.

My parents and their lawyers had come up with a ploy to "transfer" me to another psych facility closer to my home. But in actuality, the paramedics are transferring me to a local hospital near my house where doctors actually take proper care of me and my medical needs until I'm stable enough to go home.

Ha! Ha!

Take that!

But all I can truly say is . . .

Thank. You. For. Saving. Me.

On the day I left that facility, I learned that God always answers our prayers, but just not when we want or how we expect. But this timing doesn't matter, because I am saved, and I am free from the hell I'd been living in. I know the battle isn't over, but this is a good start.

The lights will eventually go completely out, but for now, I am safe with people who love me and want me to get well.

4

DARKNESS

Late August 2006 to December 2008

Darkness. In the dictionary it is defined as "absence of light, obscurity, and lack of knowledge or enlightenment." I would say that this definition perfectly sums up the time between mid-August 2006 to late December 2008. During this time, I am very frail and fragile physically and mentally. My brain is in distress, and I am in and out of various states of consciousness. At times I am lucid, but I am what many would describe as a ghost, unable to comprehend even the simplest of tasks and activities. Often, I am unaware of who I am, where I am, and who those closest to me are. I am lost, so lost. It is incredibly hard to write about this period because I honestly have little to no recollection of it. So, it'll be brief.

My life and routine are simple. Due to lack of answers and explanations, my family often just has to take it day by day.

Whichever state I am in, they just have to "roll with it." My family doesn't stop fighting for me—to find answers—and loving me unconditionally. I honestly feel bad for them. I am not living; I am merely existing. And yet they still take care of me and show me so much love and support and kindness. Most of us think, *Well, of course, that's what families do.* But I've learned that not all families do that. Most people get tired or weary, and they "can't handle it." I've heard firsthand that this phrase is more common than you realize.

Still with little to no answers, my mummy searches far and wide for a treatment or cure to get her daughter back. She loves me unconditionally and takes amazing care of me. Our family tries to be "normal" and get back to living outside of the hospital. Most of the time I'm able to be at home. My health stabilizes and does not worsen; it is somewhat of a reprieve compared to where I was not too long ago. My mummy finds various holistic healers and ways to keep my body alive and somewhat stable. Doctors are unable to determine what is causing my condition but are able to get on top of what is causing the pain. The worst pain you can possibly experience is nerve pain, and that is what my body is riddled with. After various attempts with different medicines, the doctors finally discover that all it takes is a single drug to eliminate the very thing that debilitated me in the first place. After nearly nine months, I am pain free (finally). Eliminating the pain is a relief to my family, and it definitely makes my life somewhat easier. Despite my insanely high pain tolerance, I am happy that I don't have to "tolerate" it any longer.

The pain was real.

I wasn't crazy.

Unfortunately, this "relief" period is short-lived.

Doctors have yet to diagnose or explain what is wrong with me. And so, my family live with the unknown and do their best to keep me healthy and stable. I do not know who I was, or where I was . . . I am what seems to be a two-year-old in a teenage body. People try to speak to me; friends who have known me since I was five are strangers because I am in and out of cognitive awareness. Often even my own family are strangers. I am a completely different person occupying a body full of memories and a life. Going through the motions, searching for answers, all while imprisoned in this foreign body.

I am a ghost.

Drifting.

Floating.

In a world I don't know, with a life I have no connection to.

Tests had shown that the blood vessels in my brain were inflamed but fail to give an explanation as to why or how to stop it from getting worse. Day by day the inflammation is getting worse. I am a ticking time bomb . . . and my family are sitting ducks.

Strike one.

Strike two.

Strike three.

Game over.

After about a year and a half, my body begins shutting down even more.

I'm losing . . . c, c, c, control.

M, m, m, my body is not responding.

The vise . . . is back.

Suddenly the crushing headaches return with mysterious convulsions. Each headache is followed with a seizure that feels as if I'm being struck by lightning.

Z, Z, Z, Zaaaaaaaapppppp.

"Victoria, Victoria? What are you feeling? Can you please tell Mummy?"

I'm, I'm, I'm . . .

Gone.

Desperate to keep me out of the hospital given our horrific past experiences, my mummy tries so hard to help me and take care of me. But things quickly get too bad, and we are once again rushed back to the ER. The seizures and headaches and my condition have dramatically worsened. They immediately admit me to the local hospital and start running tests. Realizing that something very serious is going on, they want to rush me to a major hospital in Massachusetts. But my parents *refuse* to go back, and so instead of going south, the decision is made to go north to a new hospital where I am immediately admitted to the pediatric intensive care unit. The seizures strike every few minutes, my heart rate sky-rockets, and I have trouble breathing. The doctors want to run several tests but need to shut my body down in order to do so, so they place me in a medically induced coma.

Darkness.

Again.

5

BREAKING FREE

January 2009

Hello?!

Nobody can hear me, but I can suddenly hear them.

I'm back.

I think I've been gone a really long time. I've somewhat managed to put the pieces of the puzzle together and figure this out. But why?

Am I crazy?

Is this a dream?

Will anyone ever hear me?

Will I be stuck like this forever?

I regularly have these awful seizures. Confusion tires my brain, and I use every moment that I'm not seizing to get my bearings. I wonder what day it is, or what month it is, and how old I am.

I know I am in the hospital but unsure for how long. Eventually, through close listening and awareness of my surroundings, I find some answers . . .

It's January . . .

2009 . . .

2009!!!

That means I am fourteen years old.

Fourteen . . .

The truth begins to slowly dawn on me. Two years have passed, two precious growing years. These are years that I will *never* get back. Years of playing field hockey, swimming, learning, developing, and—most important—living. Years of being a kid and doing kid stuff. All of a sudden, I wake up suddenly a teenager and no longer a little girl. Everything has changed, and I wasn't aware to see it happen. I have no recollection of it changing. It kind of feels like I was forced to grow up against my will and control. How could all of this time pass without me even realizing it?

Who am I?

What has become of the little girl I vaguely remember?

Will I ever get back to the life I left behind?

In an instant I remember my three brothers and my parents, and I wonder how they are. Are they okay? Have they been able to keep their sanity through this awful ordeal? Have they come to visit me . . . wherever I am?

I am coming back.

I promise.

What has happened in the world while I've been away? What have I lost while life has gone on without my participation?

Where are my friends?

What about school?

Do I even look the same?

· · ·

I fight the rising anxiety and fear and confusion and try to make sense of my situation. I need to calm down; I need to gather my thoughts and relax. Just remember . . .

I am here.

I am alive.

I know who I am.

I remember my life and my family.

Wait.

Where are they?

I cannot help but think about my three brothers; they must be so scared. I want more than anything to grab their hands and smile and tell them that I will be okay and that I'm still here. I'm not gone. And I want them to know that I'm going to fight really hard to get back to them. In some way, it may be a blessing that I can't see how I look . . . in this room. I feel pretty awful on the inside; I imagine I might look even worse on the outside. I love them so much and don't want them to be upset or scared. I can feel the tubes that are hooked up to me and can only imagine the sight they see when they visit me. But despite the sickness, I see the bright colored cards, posters, and pictures on my walls. And the butterfly balloons tied to the end of my bed. I figure out I'm in the hospital, but in many ways, my room reminds me of home.

I miss home so much.

My brothers *do* come to visit me. I'm sure now that they've been coming all along. I gradually see how each of them is handling my situation. William is the sensitive one; he always has been. Since we were little, I've taken care of him and watched out for him. From wiping his nose in kindergarten to playing street hockey, William and I have always been buddies, and I've always been his person. I've always known when he was upset, and I always knew how to help him.

He needs me now more than ever
and I can't even help him.

Every time William visits, he crawls among the wires and tubes and gives me a tender hug. He is quiet and barely says a word, and I know it's because he is upset, but he doesn't want me to know.

William, it's okay.
I'll be okay.
We'll be playing street hockey soon.
I promise.

Cameron is the outspoken one; we used to call him the Mayor. He's always been so smiley and happy and wonderful. When he feels something, he says it. Whether he's upset or happy, you always know with Cameron. But he is also strong and always positive, even during this whole time. Despite being devastated, he continually tells my mummy and me how beautiful I am. Every time he visits, he leans over my bed and pats my head and says, "Look how beautiful she is. Isn't she beautiful?"

"Beautiful" is the last word I'd use to describe how I feel.

"Brutal" is more the word of choice.

But thanks, Cammy.

Despite putting on a brave face, Cameron has his moments. Sometimes he just bursts into tears because I'm not there to "tell him not to get extra Tater Tots." My Cam has always loved Tater Tots, and when he'd get a hot lunch at school, I'd always tell him not to get extra ones because they're not good for him.

Cameron, you're allowed to have extra Tots

until I come back to school.

I'll be back, I promise.

Then there is my older brother LJ; he must be in college now. He's six years older than me, which would make him twenty by now.

Twenty.

He's an adult now.

Since day one, he has been my protector and my big brother.

LJ always watched out for us three triplets, but he seemed to have a soft spot for me. He would play dolls with me when I was little and go on the scary roller coasters with me and would always tell me, "Don't worry, Tors, I'll always protect you." When this journey began, he was only seventeen, and I later learn that he had to grow up overnight and help take care of my brothers while my parents took care of me.

There were lots of times while I was still home that I'd take a turn for the worse in the middle of the night, and my parents would rush into LJ's room telling him that he needed to get up and watch the boys and make sure they get to school. Then we would bolt to the ER, and LJ would be left wondering if I was going to come back home. Nonetheless, he kept plugging away at school and being strong for me and our family. But there were times when he couldn't: one day he fell over the end of my bed, crying the most painful cry, and asked Mummy, "Is she going to die?"

I'm so sorry, LJ.

No big brother should bear that cross.

I'm going to fight.

I promise.

We will get through this.

LJ is the one I worry most about. He was on his own at school and had to be a grown-up overnight. I'm sure he had his own struggles, like every other teenager, yet he had to keep going and keep fighting—oftentimes without my mum and dad, because they were with me. I pray for LJ often, asking God to watch over him. And God answered that prayer in the form of his girlfriend, Liz. She is his rock and cares very much for him and gives him strength. Not only does she care about LJ, she cares about all of us. Liz is selfless and kind and always there for my brother, my family, and me. She goes above and beyond, and at times keeps everyone together and strong. We are all fighting, and Liz has joined the army.

Thank you, Liz.
You don't really know me,
but I've gotten to know you.
I love you and cannot thank you enough.
And LJ . . . you better marry that girl.
(Never thought I'd ever approve of a girl for LJ.
I'm super protective of him.)

My three brothers are so selfless and strong that at times it leaves me speechless. (Obviously, I am already speechless externally, but they amaze me so much that I am speechless on the inside, too.) Our parents didn't raise us to be weak, but going through these years with me must be incredibly scary and horrific. They are so strong at such young ages. Their strength gives me strength.

They are fighting . . . for me.
Living . . . for me.
Believing . . . in me.

I guess none of us realizes how strong we are until being strong is all we have left. My family's strength never wavers. Of course, I know they are tired and scared and terrified of a future without me, but they never let me know that. Although they cannot see any sign that I am here, they refused to believe that I am gone.

Life kept going.

Even in the worst of times, my family maintains an overflowing joy and love that daily fills my room. I always have a stellar manicure and pedicure, the coolest "trendy" clothes (thank you, William), and exceptional care.

I am still me, just a little different version.

But I am here.

I am alive.

And I am with my family.

And they love me . . . I love them.

And love conquers all.

Knowing that my family loves me so faithfully and fiercely temporarily eases my anxiety and fear. I am not completely gone, and I have my sanity and brain function. I can work with that, and I can live with that. Although nobody else knows that I'm in there, at least I know I'm here. And my family isn't leaving me or giving up on me.

This is a fight.

And it's not near over.

In contrast to my family's steadfast hope, the doctors, nurses, and specialists always enter my room with somber faces. Their reports are grim, and my future does not look so bright in their eyes. I hear them tell my family:

"It's too late."

"There is nothing we can do."

"Most likely, she will not come out of this."

"You have to prepare for the possibility of her dying."

"If she does survive, she will not be able to walk, talk, eat, or move, and she'll require constant care."

They have no idea that I can hear *everyone* and *everything.*

I'M STILL HERE!!!!

I'm here, and I'm terrified.

I don't want to die.

Please don't let me die.

I haven't even had the opportunity to live yet.

In my mind, I'm at Lake Winnipesaukee, my favorite place in the world. I'm at my absolute favorite spot on the water. It is known as the Broads, and it is the largest part of the lake. The view is breathtaking; the sun is shining over the water, causing it to sparkle. Majestic mountains tower in the distance. The wind blows, and I can even feel my hair tickle my face. I'm on the boat with my family. We are happy, smiling, and laughing—something we were not too long ago. For just a moment—a small but incredibly powerful moment—everything is perfect, and I'm *okay.*

These daydreams become my refuge and my lifeline. A reminder that there is a life worth fighting for outside these hospital walls, and outside this painful prison I am trapped in. My dreams vary from day to day. Sometimes I'm a reporter at the X Games, or a movie actress, or skiing out west, or running—fast and far away from my hospital room. Other days, I'm dancing on my favorite TV show, *Dancing with the Stars*. I can picture the sparkly costumes, high heels, and the various dances. I've always loved to dance, and I want more than anything to be able to twirl and hear music and have that freedom. I also write screenplays in my mind, creating stories and characters that intrigue me and distract me. I prepare for the life I want to live beyond this hospital bed.

Instead of focusing on my pain, I focus on my will to live and to be someone someday. I focus on living and being able to one day do all of those things. Because if I focus on where I am now, I don't know how long I will last. I have to keep envisioning the life and the exciting adventures that await me. Each day that I get through these horrific, painful seizures and migraines that have violently taken over my body, I am one step closer to breaking free and living the incredible life I've envisioned. So, I often run away from the negative thoughts that try to take over my brain. I have only my own thoughts and time to think. Plenty of time to think.

Keep dreaming.

Keep believing.

To avoid continuing down the path of negative thinking—

which gets really scary really fast—I decide to fill my mind with everything I am grateful for.

Now, you're probably thinking . . .

WHAT could I possibly be grateful for?

My life has completely fallen apart, and I lie here trapped inside my own body. Fighting the good fight each day. Constantly fighting the pull to give up. Yet, in spite of the "hopeless" prognosis I often hear, I am able to find plenty of things to be grateful for. Starting with the simple fact that my mind is now working enough that I can reflect. And the more I think, the more the list grows.

I'm not dead . . . right ? That's a BIG win!

It might seem that starting with "I'm not dead" is really scraping the bottom of the barrel—and hey, that may be true! But it's a start—a good start—and it was one for the top of the list. Then I begin to think how that simple hospital room has turned into a makeshift "home." And when I'm stable, my parents create a hospital at our home. Whether in the hospital or at home, each place is bursting with love. I have this amazing, dedicated family around me day and night, and they are 100 percent committed to my every need.

But reality frequently smacks me across the face, and it is sometimes really hard to be grateful. I'm a prisoner inside my own body. Everything is disconnected—my body doesn't feel like it belongs to me. I try to wiggle a finger, nothing. I try to move my eyes to see out the window, nothing. All I can do is stare straight ahead. I have no control over my eyes, and my vision oftentimes is distorted. I try to open my mouth and scream, nothing. It feels as if I'm being constantly electrocuted. I will later learn that my nerves are misfiring due to my lack of movement, and that there is a war raging inside my nervous system, spinal cord, and brain.

Breathe.

Just breathe.

Find your place, go to the lake.

Forget, just forget, for one moment.

Breathe, I know it hurts, but breathe.

But when seizures strike, I can't breathe, my body convulses, machines beep, and I feel as if I'm being struck by lightning. I want to pass out and escape this torture, but I can't do anything except bear the pain. As the seizure subsides, my heart races and my head spins. My body relentlessly fights against me. It is a vicious, violent, and horrific cycle. I'm continually pulled underwater, never reaching the surface.

How can I live like this?

How can I break out of this prison?

I need a miracle.

Please, God.

I need a miracle.

6

AWAKE . . . AND BACK TO HELL

September 2009 to November 2009

All I need is something—anything—that can show the ones around me that I am still in here. But the seizures are relentless, and I rarely have a "break" when I can try to give some sort of sign. In spite of my strong will to live, my hope is dwindling. And my will to live was running on empty.

It can't get much worse than this.

It's my fifteenth birthday—September 26—and my family has decorated my room with balloons and cards and even sung "Happy Birthday" to me. But the day is far from happy. I sense that everyone feels deflated and exhausted. It's been almost four years since birthdays were considered a "happy" time in my family.

Will I make it to my next birthday?

Though I am still gravely ill, and the seizures continue to ravage me, my parents wanted me home. The doctors have done all they can and have little to no hope for my recovery. "Lost cause" is an ongoing theme. My family—as strong as they are—is weary. And I am weary of trying and sick of being so sick. Aside from being at home in a makeshift hospital room in our living room, there isn't much reason for hope. I look at my birthday as another year trapped, another year watching the world go on without me.

But today, on my birthday, I receive a visit from someone who reignites my hope.

"In time, she will be healed," says Father Bashobora. As I listen to the conversations around me, I learn that countless people around the world are praying for me and that word about my desperate situation has spread.

A woman from a local church heard my story and passed it along to Father Bashobora, a spiritual healer who was coming into town to speak and heal at a local church. Father Bashobora heals thousands all over the world, and when he heard my story, he asked if I could come to the church, so he could pray with me. The woman explained the situation and that I was not stable enough to leave my hospital bed. So, he decided to make a house call.

Father Bashobora does not normally make house calls. But now, on my fifteenth birthday, he's here to pray with my family and me. At this point, seizures are striking every two to five minutes, so I am going in and out of convulsions and cannot always hear what Father Bashobora is saying. But I can feel immense love and light, and I know deep down that it is a gift from God. He keeps saying, "In time, she will be healed." His words are the first words of hope my family and I have heard in a very long time. Everyone else speaks of sorrow and sadness and is afraid to offer hope that may not be realized.

What we need is a miracle. We desperately need a ray of hope.

Not long after his visit, my health declines significantly and the seizures become even worse. My parents once again rush me to the new hospital and I am admitted. No longer stable for at-home hospital care. Out of options, the doctors at the new hospital begin to go down the "crazy" route . . . *again*. I am frustrated but my parents are frustrated beyond belief, and we are once again fighting this battle. Despite abnormal scans and very obvious neurological deficits, I am still being dismissed as crazy by one "expert." It seems that when doctors have *no* clue as to how to help you or what is wrong, they assume you are crazy. Unfortunately, this "crazy" label has followed me everywhere. *Everywhere.*

I just wanna go home.

No more hospitals.

Please.

During my lengthy stay I'm eventually diagnosed with transverse myelitis (TM), a neurological condition that causes inflammation and damage to the spinal cord. When the nerve cells are damaged, your body can't send messages to other areas. The gravity of my situation prevents my family from being able to continue the in-home hospital care. The new medical team agrees that I need to be placed in a rehabilitation center for constant care. My mother is tired, and they urge her to take a break. The seizures have not improved and continue to spiral out of control.

I am a "lost cause."

There is nothing more that can be done.

So, I am sent to a rehab facility in New Hampshire, a place I had been treated back in the earlier days of this journey. My first experience here was pleasant, so surely, this one will be a good experience too.

But from the moment I arrive in late fall, I have a bad feeling. I'm afraid—actually, I'm terrified.

Something doesn't feel right.

The nurses urge my mother to take a break and "get some rest."

Please don't leave me here.

But she stays and meets with the nurses, doctors, and therapists. When talking with my mum, they sound nice and caring, but I don't like how much they are pushing her to leave me to go to a house across the street where families of patients can stay. Also, because I have a roommate in my room, they use it as a reason my mummy cannot stay. My mother has not left my side during any of my recent hospital stays; she has been with me constantly. Looking out for me and being my voice and advocate. I'm completely defenseless and vulnerable, and she's always been my voice and protector. Knowing she is still there, I am less concerned. Until . . .

Where have you gone?

I awake the first night to find that my mother is gone. She was lying beside me when I fell asleep. I assume that she finally listened to the medical team and left to get some rest at the nearby on-campus house for family members. I begin to panic.

No, no, no.

I know my mummy is exhausted and needs time to regroup and sleep. A part of me understands why she left me, but another part of me resents her for leaving me. I didn't realize that the doctors and nurses were preventing her from staying with me 24/7. And I also didn't realize it, but during the few hours she was not with me, she was doing everything she could to help me. Visiting with outside-of-the-box healers and creating a game plan to get me stronger. She was searching everywhere for help. The only problem was, I had no idea, so I was angry. When I should've been thankful. I guess that's sometimes what makes life so crazy. You could be going through absolute hell and think you are alone when the ones you love most—who you think have left you—are fighting harder than they've ever fought to help you. That was what my mummy was doing, fighting to get me better.

Keep fighting.

The nurses and LNAs (licensed nursing assistants) and therapists quickly become condescending, aggressive, and mean. They mock me and call me "crazy," "waste of space," "crybaby," "hypochondriac," "stupid," "ugly," and "useless," to name a few of their insults. (Doing my best to keep this book PG, there were a few words used that cannot be repeated.) They hit me and abruptly move me, inflicting pain while saying demeaning and hurtful things to my face. I try to cry out in pain, but they restrain my arms because of my seizures. They secure the restraints so tightly that I lose feeling and circulation in my fingers.

Help, somebody, help me!

Please!

Never have I wanted so much to talk and scream. When my family comes to visit, the nurses and LNAs quickly switch gears and act caring and adoring and tell them how I'm "doing so well." On the inside, I'm screaming louder than I've ever screamed.

Please help!

They are lying!

Don't listen to them!

PLEASE!

Not only do I feel physically and verbally mistreated, but I am also being neglected. The nurses often neglect to tend to my bladder needs, leaving me feeling like my bladder is going to explode. My feeding pump is hooked up to the wrong port, causing my stomach to spasm and me to vomit uncontrollably. And instead of cleaning me up and helping me, I am left lying in my own vomit.

My mother visits me every day, but she is completely clueless about what is going on. When she is there, the nurses, LNAs and therapists are on their best behavior. But when she is not there, which is usually later in the evening or sometimes during the day, all hell breaks loose. I was used to feeling frustrated, but the fierce anger I feel toward my mum is new, and I want to just *scream* at her.

Why have you left me here?!

Don't you know what they are doing to me?!

I've never really been angry at anyone before—except for "F" at the unmarked facility. And I never imagined that I'd ever be angry at the one person I love the most, my mummy. But I am so fed up with my situation and with the abuse that in my mind I lash out at her. She hasn't done anything wrong except get some much-needed sleep. And it's not even her choice to not be here. She wants to be, but the nurses won't let her. All of this pent-up frustration finally boils over—and I am *angry*!

I'm done.

With everything.

So . . . in my anger, I begin to give up. I quit dreaming about things to come, and I can't find the energy to be grateful. Instead, I feel like a victim, which is a horrible feeling of violation and helplessness. I'm being hurt over and over again, and I can't fight back or tell anyone.

I scream in my head at God as I am relentlessly abused. Faith had always been my refuge, but I cannot find the faith to keep fighting anymore. Instead, I am angry at everything and everyone—especially God.

How could you allow this to continue?

Make it stop, please!

Can you even hear me?

Why have you left me, God?

This anger is uncomfortable and unnerving, but it fuels my despair and my desperate desire to die.

I can't take this anymore.

I'm done.

Good-bye.

Let me go.

One day blurs into the next. When my family visits, they wonder why tears stream down my face and I seem agitated. The nurses come up with preposterous reasons as to why this could be and continue to mislead them. I don't even want to look at my family. Even though it's not their fault, I'm still angry at them. I'm angry at everything and everyone.

Please just go away.

Please.

I don't want to see any of you.

Leave me alone.

But even though I'm mad at my family, seeing them makes it harder to give up and go. Their love and fight keep me stuck between leaving and staying.

I gradually detach from the world and my family. Internally, I'm preparing to die. I'm getting ready to leave this world and everyone I love. I can't do this anymore—I *refuse* to do this anymore. I've got nothing left. I just pray that my death is quick and painless, which seems unlikely, given how much pain I'm already in. Every time I close my eyes, I pray that I never wake up. I pray that God will be merciful and take me away from this hell that I am trapped in.

Please just take me away.

Please.

Sleep has been elusive throughout this journey. Nighttime is not my friend. My frequent seizures steal the rest I desperately need. The only way I get any reprieve is when my body eventually passes out from sheer exhaustion. But every time I wake, I am discouraged to find that I am still here.

One night, someone else seems intent on making my prayer to die a reality.

On this night, I am abruptly awakened from my sleep by a fierce seizure. The shocking pain and violent convulsions take over my body. As the seizure subsides, I'm bewildered and try to bring my body back to rest so I can get a few more hours of sleep and be away from the world a little longer. My eyes close, and I begin to drift off and I pray . . .

Please just let me go.

God, have mercy and end this now.

Please.

Suddenly, I hear a rustling noise from across the room. Before I have time to get my bearings, two hands take hold of my neck. The mysterious hands begin to squeeze and shake me and force my body back. My head whips back and forth as the air is slowly constricted from my chest, and I feel an extreme drowning sensation. My chest writhes in a desperate search for oxygen. I try to scream, to no avail.

H...E...L...P...

I want to move, but I can't. I want to pull these hands away from my throat, but I'm trapped. I try to stay conscious, but my eyeballs feel as if they're going to pop out of their sockets. Then I hear a searing, hissing female voice say, "I'm going to f***ing kill you," over and over and over again, like a possessed mantra.

She's going to kill me.

As her grip tightens, her hissing becomes louder and more profound. Although I'd wished for death just moments before, I am now desperate for something—anything—to free me from the stronghold. My heart races, and my body writhes and convulses in search of oxygen.

Air!

I NEED air!

Just when I think I can't take any more, I'm filled with a strange peace. I stop fighting and my body begins to relax as I ready myself for death. I am completely calm.

Go ahead, do it.

End it.

Please.

I can't do this anymore.

Please, just let me be free.

From EVERYTHING.

I've got nothing left.

I begin to welcome death like the friend I met a few years ago. Enough is enough. I can't help but think that this is the answer to the prayer I've been praying for a long time. I'm so ready to be free, and it seems that death is my only way out. Survival means being a prisoner, and dying means breaking free from the prison that has held me captive for nearly three and a half years. Back in the unmarked facility, I fought the desire to die, but now there is no more fight in me. All of the pain and suffering and inability to defend myself have finally caught up to me. For once, I am taking control and am ready for things to end. Right now, in this moment of immense struggle I am alone, fed up with suffering, and not afraid. I feel that I have said my good-byes to my family. I do not want to fight or live any longer.

I just want to . . .

BREATHE!

Suddenly the grip loosens, and I gasp for air as if I'd never breathed before. As my body tries to recover, my eyes open just in time to get a glimpse of the person who nearly killed me. She strangely resembles a rag doll, but much rougher looking. Her hair is in one of my favorite hairstyles—two French braids. I never imagined that the hairstyle I loved so much would be on the head of someone trying to kill me.

Within a blink she is gone.

I'll never know what made that woman do what she did or why she let go and left. But I've learned an important lesson:

Trust no one.

I know I have a family and people who love me, but this is not right. This is no way to spend birthdays, Christmas, and my teenage years. It finally hits me: I'm watching the world go on without me. People are growing up and forgetting. Forgetting about me wasting away in a hospital bed. This is no way to live. I want to be free! This prison has consumed my life, and I'm beginning to forget what it was like to live. This is no life. I used to do a lot of fun things. I used to be free! And now . . . I am losing myself.

Who am I?

What am I?

Where have you gone, Victoria?

I feel myself falling deeper and deeper in an ocean of despair. I struggle to get to the surface, but I am continually pulled under. The waves are too much, and I can't swim. I cannot reach the surface; I'm drowning.

I want to be free.

My daydreams are fading. It's been a long time since I was able to drift away to my place on the lake. Four years earlier, I fought against my wish to die, but I don't even have the little strength I had back then. I've got nothing left.

I'm caught between dying and surviving. I can feel my body shutting down. Finally, I can be at peace. Finally, I can be free . . .

WAIT.

. . . I see my mum; her arms are outstretched, and she is smiling. My dad and brothers are next to her doing the same. I'm standing in front of them, and there is a car next to me. I look at the car and begin to walk toward it. All I can think of is, *Finally, I can leave this place and be free from this pain.* But, then I look back at my family. Their smiles have gone, and they are crying. I see my triplet brothers William and Cameron. We are the three musketeers and wombmates, and we do everything together. I see my big brother LJ, my protector. He would often carry my limp body around when I needed to be moved. When things got scary, he was there, even though he was scared, too. My dad is crying, too. I'm his little girl, and he can't help me. Then I look back at my mum, the strongest woman I know. She has been relentless in helping me, never once giving up. She falls to her knees and cries uncontrollably.

Don't go.

Hold on, Victoria.

I snap back to reality and realize that this daydream could become reality if I were to go. How could I be so selfish? Not once have any of my family even thought about giving up on me. For the last four years, they have done everything to give me the best life possible. They've cared for me so tenderly, and my mum has even made sure that my nails were done. Although this life is far from ideal, it is still a life, a life worth living.

Hold on.

There is a life worth living.

So, I make a choice—an incredibly challenging choice. *LIVE.* Regardless of the situation, just live. I wanted to give up; I wanted to die. But I couldn't, I couldn't go; I wasn't done on Earth yet. So, I make a promise:

"If I get a second chance to live, I promise I will make it count. I will not waste even one moment. And I will do more than just live; I will change the world."

I make this promise to God. He is the only one who can hear me. Sometimes, it is in our darkest moments that we realize the most powerful things. And we are often tested the most severely right before the miracle.

I can't give up.

I've come too far.

I've fought too hard.

In some ways, I feel happy that the woman didn't kill me and I didn't die. But I'm not going to lie: a small part of me is disappointed.

Now, when my mother visits, I try every way I can to communicate to her, but all she can see is that I'm agitated and upset. She cannot understand why, and that only frustrates me more.

Get me out of here!

I continually try to tell her this, but to her and the rest of the world my desperate cry for help sounds like mumbles and jumbled agitation.

Please, Mummy, hear me!

One afternoon, my mum steps out of the room for a few minutes. My restraint isn't strapped, and so when a seizure strikes, my left hand plunges into my forehead. The seizure quickly subsides, but the LNA grabs my left hand and uses my own hand to punch myself in the face. Each punch sends shooting pain to my hand and face, and I cry out. Over and over again, until I'm finally able to release a blood-curdling scream that makes the LNA step back in horror. My mummy runs into the room yelling, "What is going on? What have you done?" The nurse shakes her head and tries to act as if nothing were wrong.

"Get out!" my mum yells.

Mummy, please save me.

Tears run down my face, and Mum crawls into bed with me. "Don't worry, Mummy is here, and I'm not going anywhere."

7

BLINK OF HOPE

November 2009 to August 2010

The doctors' efforts to stop my seizures begin to intensify after that incident. Ever since the unmarked facility, my mummy makes the decision to stay with me. The nurses and LNAs are again on their "best" behavior. They seem to know that my mum is paying extra-close attention to their interactions with me. One wrong word or move, and my mummy will know. I imagine they are praying I never get my voice back. Because if I do, they'll be in a *lot* of trouble.

In an effort to help me sleep, a doctor prescribes a popular sleep medication. It does not put me to sleep, but my body becomes calm. It relaxes me, and my seizures are much less frequent. My face even relaxes into a slight smile, which has not been present for quite some time. For the first time, I am not fighting against a seizure and my body is not fighting against me.

Ahh . . . freedom, finally.

A chemical in the sleeping medication has somehow interrupted the neurotransmitter that causes my seizures. For the first time in a year, I am relaxed and not in pain. My headache goes away, and I'm free. Free to try harder to break out of this prison that is my body.

I need a miracle.

A true miracle.

But miracles are hard to come by.

Please, God.

Blink, blink, blink.

Wait.

I'm blinking!

I'm blinking!

One blink, double blink, triple blink!

Now let's try something tricky, look left, now right. YES!

My eyes!

I have control of my eyes back!

I'm no longer just staring blankly.

Mum!

Mum!

Oh, wait, I don't have my voice yet.

Mum, Mum, where are you? I want to see you!

My mum walks into my room and begins to get everything ready for bed. I lock my eyes onto her. I follow her around the room. I can see the world outside the windows. Oh, how beautiful it is. The trees are brown; it must be close to winter. The sun is so bright and beautiful. I've missed this bright, beautiful world.

Focus, Victoria.

Back to Mum: I need to see her see me seeing her. Never in my life have I been so focused. She walks over, and her eyes meet mine. I don't lose my focus. I'm locked in on her eyes. She sees me, finally, she sees me!

I'm still here, Mummy.

I keep my gaze, and I focus. I can feel a difference in my eyes. The glossed-over stare is gone. I'm focused. I'm cognitive, and I'm ready to connect with my mamma. She takes a step back, and I keep staring at her. She sees me, and I see her.

"Victoria?"

I keep my focus locked in.

"If you can hear me, blink twice."

Blink . . .

"Come on, Victoria, one more . . ."

Blink.

Over and over again.

And that little thing that we take for granted, that everyone has done many times while reading this book, became my lifeline. Suddenly, I had a way to communicate: one blink for yes, two blinks for no. Instantly, my mummy burst into tears of joy, the weight of the world was lifted from her back, and it is undoubtedly the single most powerful moment I have ever shared with anyone.

"Victoria is in there."

That was the moment of relief for my family. Finally, they knew that I was still there. Although horrified that I was locked in, they were so happy that I was responsive.

• • •

My world has opened up in the simplest of ways, and I couldn't be happier. For most people, blinking isn't a big deal or relevant, but for me, it is my passport back into the world of the living, and to let everyone know . . .

I'm still here.

All of a sudden, I can see and communicate. I no longer feel like I am fading away and missing the world around me. A simple miracle has reignited the fire and fight that had been slowly disappearing. My eyes—having control of my eyes—have made me one of the happiest humans on Earth. I can move my eyes and see my family and the world around me.

Thank you, God.

When I'm not having seizures, I can focus and communicate. Not worrying about losing consciousness is one of the biggest reliefs. Each day, the seizures become less and less frequent. I can feel the sparkle returning to my eyes and spirit.

LOCKED IN

• • •

I am alive, and I am stable, and I am able to be at home with my family. Now that my seizures are under control and I am medically stable, the doctors allow me to come home. My whole family breathes a sigh of relief.

My brothers like taking me around the house in my wheelchair, and my mum begins to bring me up to speed on what's been happening in our family and the world.

I can't yet talk, but I've found ways of communicating. Through blinking and raw sounds, my family always seems to know what I need. I am slowly regaining movement in my arms, but my hands are still clenched due to extreme spasticity. I haven't used my arms in quite a while, so moving them is far from graceful but gets the job done. But with this newfound progress in my arms, I'm able to expand my communication through a communication board which is a sheet with lots of various pictures that each represent something I need or want to say.

My family continues to amaze me with their love and kindness and support. Although I am still significantly compromised, they treat me like a normal human being. I am included in every conversation and never left out. I become my mummy's buddy, and she brings me along everywhere she goes. One day in particular she brings me to one of my favorite places, the beach. We breathe in the fresh air, and I am truly at peace.

77

Driving back, my mum looks back at me in the rearview mirror, and she says something I will *never* forget. "I want you to know that if nothing else comes back and you don't get any better, Mummy will always be there for you and take care of you." This woman never ceases to amaze me. That comment means the world to me and is so incredibly sweet, but I have other plans.

I will not only survive,

I will thrive.

As I improve, I am more aware of the world around me and the life I've missed out on for the last four years. A *lot* has changed since I was eleven. Now, fifteen years old, I want to return to my old normalcy, yet I wonder if I will ever be truly normal again.

And when I see myself in the mirror for the first time, I am taken aback. I don't remember seeing myself in a mirror during the four years since I started getting sick. And today, I don't recognize the face looking back at me.

Who are you?

Where is Victoria?

I cannot help but see the flaws, there are so many of them.

I truly need to cut myself a break after all I've been through, but the superficial reflection of me does not "measure up" to who I think I should be. A lot changes from age eleven to fifteen. I also hadn't realized that all of the side effects from various medications would affect the way I look. My face is puffy, my teeth are crooked, I have an odd haircut with bangs, and I even have boobs, which is a drastic change in itself. I am discouraged, and the thought of being normal and pretty and in shape and back to myself seems like a far-out pipe dream. I don't know what to do or what to be or what would become of me.

Will I ever talk again?

Sit up on my own?

Eat?

Walk?

Write?

Go to school?

Live independently?

Have a boyfriend?

Be in shape?

Move?

Be strong?

My ongoing list of uncertainties and insecurities keep me up at night. I struggle constantly with fear . . . of *everything*. I am afraid to sleep because I don't know what I will wake up to.

Will the seizures come back?

Will I get sick again?

Be trapped again?

Will my world be taken away from me again?

I don't understand it at the time, but I am experiencing severe post-traumatic stress, and my brain is on overload. When I was sick and fighting for my life, I hadn't struggled with fear. But now,

I am afraid *all* the time. The world has gone on for four years without me being a part of it. And so, the world seems scary, and I feel that I don't belong. I crave the simple eleven-year-old life I left behind four years ago. But that life is gone. That Victoria is gone. I am a new Victoria, and I have to figure out how to adapt accordingly. I honestly have no idea how to live "normally" and just be a kid. I don't know what to do.

How can I live a normal life?

The trauma and darkness that have plagued my last few years have now come to the surface and are tormenting me. Let's just say, nobody gives me a "How to Cope with Losing Four Years of Your Life" manual (maybe that should be my next book). I am also dealing with a bit of agoraphobia (an anxiety disorder that takes the form of fear of crowded spaces) because I haven't been out in the world for so long. Everything has changed. For example, I wake up to discover that everyone else my age is focused on iPhones and Facebook.

I don't even know what they are.

Frankly, I don't know what anything is anymore.

• • •

The next few months are a blur of doctor visits and physical, occupational, and speech therapy sessions. Little by little, I am returning to routine family life and regaining some of the function I had lost. I try to find my "new normal." But this normal is more complicated and requires a lot of work! Getting out of the house and going to the bathroom are way more complicated than they were before all this. It amazes me how hard it is to accomplish even the simplest of tasks such as wiggling a finger, holding a pencil, saying hello (*H* is a hard letter to master), and holding my head up. I still have issues with my stomach, and so I've had to learn how to operate my GJ (gastrostomy-jejunostomy) tube pump, which continuously pumps nutrition into my body. It feels as if I am climbing mountain after mountain. And just when I think I am at the top, another larger mountain materializes.

But I am determined. I want to move on with my life as much as possible and attempt to be a "normal" fifteen-year-old. As difficult as things are, I never think about giving up—not ever. I have turned into a machine, determined to "make up for lost time." I refuse to sit back and "wait" for things to come back; so instead, I force them to return. When I'm not doing physical, occupational, or speech therapy, I am moving and working hard at accomplishing the "goals" that are set for each week.

I don't just want to learn how to say a word; I want to speak concise and educated sentences. I have so much I want to say, and I want it to sound fantastic when I say it. I want to speak as if I never stopped. And I don't just want to wiggle a finger; I want complete function in my hands. Due to extreme spasticity, my arms and hands have been clenched for a few years. But thanks to twenty-two Botox injections in each arm, my clenched fists have started to release. I do not give my hands much time to recoup before I force them to do crafts and practice writing my name in cursive. I don't just want to hold my head up; I want to be able to sit up. And last, I want to transfer myself in and out of my wheelchair independently.

Wheelchair.

I never really had a chance to grieve the loss of my mobility and my new reality of being wheelchair-bound. I remember losing the use of my legs when I first got sick, but I never imagined they would be gone for good. According to the doctors, the use of my legs is not going to return, and a wheelchair will be my way of getting around for the rest of my life. That is not an easy pill to swallow.

You are far from free.

You may never be free.

My life is still far from being completely free. I want so badly to be able to move around in my wheelchair, eat, and go to the bathroom independently. In my mind I feel "fine," but severe muscle atrophy and neurological deficits continually remind me that I am not "fine."

How do I move forward?

Will I ever be okay?

I try to focus on how far I've come, and I desperately try *not* to think about how far I have to go. If I focus on that, I will quickly become incredibly depressed. And I know that depression would be a slippery slope for me. I know deep down that my life will never be how it was before I got sick, but I try to picture a wonderful and free life ahead of me. I know that the odds of having the life I imagine are not great—but who knows? We serve an almighty God who can do the impossible.

And in my case the impossible looked like, of all things, hockey.

I'll never forget the day I went to Northeast Passage the summer before I started high school. Northeast Passage is an adaptive sports program out of the University of New Hampshire. I'd heard of NEP back in February right around the time of the Vancouver Olympics, as I slowly was coming out of my vegetative state. My mummy had gone to UNH, and the February 2010 newsletter had a whole feature on sled hockey. I knew in that moment that I wanted to get back out on the ice and back into sports. Sled hockey is specifically for players with physical limitations so instead of standing up to skate, they sit in a device known as a "sled." They use sticks with sharp pics at the bottom to propel themselves.

Before I could even talk, I let my family know that I wanted to get back on the ice in a sled. My daddy is a big-time hockey guy and has coached and played on all levels—including professionally. So, when my daddy finds out I want to get back on the ice, he is the first person to get me into a sled.

I am still *very* compromised. My arms don't work, and I can only speak a handful of words—and that is just when my muscles choose to cooperate. But I can communicate, in my own way, what I need. Daddy straps a helmet onto my head and duct-tapes sled hockey sticks in my hands, and then he takes me out for a spin. While all the other parents and family members are skating timidly and nicely with their children, my daddy is pretending to check me into the boards. Over and over again, he says, "If you're gonna play hockey, you need to be able to take a hit." My poor mummy is traumatized as she watches from the stands. My brother William penguin slides next to me and pretends to check me as well. I love every moment of it. The ice, the sticks in my hands—they remind me of me and of the passion we share as a family. Growing up at this particular rink, none of us in a million years would have imagined I would be here in a sled and we would have gone through all we had just been through. But we can't look back and think about the sadness and the loss. We have to focus on the future and the fact that I am alive and that we are slowly finding stability and peace in our new normal. It isn't perfect by any standards, but it is good, so good.

When I get into that sled, the competitive drive that I've had since birth is reignited. And being back on the ice with my family is beyond healing. I now have a place where I can be an athlete and compete—something I have missed. Sled hockey is not a sport for the fainthearted. It's an intense game, and I am doing it with two sticks that have sharp pics at the end. Many of its stars have gone through difficult struggles, so there is a lot of *heart* in the game, but it's also extremely intense.

Get back in the game.

• • •

I've always been the kind of girl who likes to play with the boys, and sled hockey is not a big girls' sport. So, in the fall of 2010, seven months after first being strapped in a sled, I join the Northeast Passage sled hockey team. The guys I play with push me and motivate me. I have to take the hard hits, and I have to learn to skate fast in order to avoid the hits. I learn about camaraderie and that I am not alone. Many of my teammates have been through horrific ordeals like me. Even though we all have different situations, we all have a story. Hearing their stories and seeing their independence and their determination to rise above their circumstances is a great encouragement to me.

Before I joined this team, I felt so alone and like nobody understood me. I struggled to fit in and feel "normal." Not only do these guys understand, they have a sick sense of humor about it. We are all sick of being called "inspirations," and we just want to be hockey players. Even if it is just for the time we spend practicing and playing, in those few hours, we are hockey players—nothing more, nothing less. We are not patients, victims, hurt, or damaged. Our battle scars are hidden by gear, and our hockey skills speak for themselves. No pity party and definitely no "taking it easy."

For the first time in a really, really long time, I can unhook my feeding tube, get out of my wheelchair, and play a game I have loved since I was a little girl. Little by little, I'm finding the Victoria I thought was lost and long gone.

Hockey saves me in many ways, but the most important thing it saves is my relationship with my dad. To be honest, while I was so sick, my relationship with him was, in many ways, broken. He struggled with my illness because he couldn't help me, and as a result, he sometimes took out his frustration on me. When I was in the throes of my illness I wanted nothing to do with him. But I quickly realized: Who am I to judge? What happened was horrific.

That's not a way to live.

I love you, Dad.

I always have.

And I always will.

Now that I'm finding myself again, I want to have a better relationship with him. When someone hurts me, my first coping method is to hide away from that person; it's my go-to defense mechanism. It may be a single word or one wrong look, and boom, I'm in my shell. I am in my shell with Daddy and have been for quite a few years. I know he loves me more than anything, but he wasn't always there when I was sick. But through a lot of prayer I learn that sometimes we hurt the people we love the most.

And sometimes, when other people are hurting, they don't realize that they are hurting us. He wasn't a bad person; he was broken and hurting and trying to keep our family together. I'm not a parent, and I can't even imagine the frustration and pain of not being able to help your child. I've always been Daddy's little girl and he has always protected me, and he couldn't during this ordeal, and that broke him.

I start to see my dad in a more positive light, as he goes out of his way to take me to hockey practice. He even helps coach our team. It is quite funny to see this hockey guy, who has grown up around stand-up skaters, try to coach a team of guys who are in sleds. He occasionally slips up and says things like, "Move your feet!" to our goalie, who has no legs. Our goalie responds with, "Yeah, thanks a lot, coach." Needless to say, the banter at times is quite hysterical. But my dad is an incredible coach, and I have seen him transform players and goalies into high-caliber athletes—some even achieving the impossible and making it to the NHL.

My dad is an amazing coach for me. He pushes me and encourages me to go further and to be faster and better than I was yesterday. He is not easy on me by any means, and if anything, he pushes me a little harder than everyone else. But it is all in love. He knew, even before I did, what I am capable of. Feeling his confidence was profoundly encouraging. For many years doctors have told me all the things I'd never be able to do, but now the tables are turned, and I discover that there is so much I *can* and *would* do.

Dad and I are now spending a lot of time together—on the ice and going to tournaments. I start to get to know him again and slowly begin to see that he is trying to be better and make up for the past. Our relationship isn't restored overnight, but this is a big start.

Keep going.

Get stronger.

Keep challenging yourself.

In addition to Daddy, Tom Carr—who is the head coach of our team—believes in me from the very start. He encourages me on the ice and challenges me to be better. He is the one who pushes my dad to get involved, too. Tom brings so much out of me when I'm on the ice. Even when we first met and while I was still having trouble sitting up, he never once treats me like a patient. I am *always* an athlete to him.

Tom also can see that I am more than a hockey player, and he constantly encourages me to explore other sports. But for now, I just want to be a hockey player—that's enough for me. But Tom doesn't give up. He knows I am a swimmer and a good one, probably better at swimming than at hockey. Swimming would offer more opportunities than hockey, and Tom keeps pushing me to explore it. He sometimes laughs and says I am like Happy Gilmore, claiming to be a hockey player when in fact I am a better swimmer.

After much back-and-forth and a lot of convincing, I get back to the water.

Never truly realizing how big of a splash I would make . . .

8

THE SPOTLIGHT OF SUCCESS

August 2010 to September 2011

Splash!

Before I know it, I am being thrown into the pool by my brothers William and Cameron. The water is *freezing,* and since I have not been in the water in many years, I am terrified. I feel awkward and disconnected from a place that has always been *my place*—ever since I was a baby. The place that once gave me the greatest peace is now the place I fear most.

When I was a kid, you'd always find me in the water. I was the first to jump in and the last to get out. Our family was always around pools and lakes. As soon as spring started to become summer, I was in the water. During the winter months, I swam competitively.

When I was just five, I started begging my mom to please let me swim on a swim team. Knowing the commitment and long days required—she was a swimmer in college—my mummy didn't let me join a team until I was nine. She wanted me to explore other sports and be a kid.

I loved the freedom and the high I got being underwater. The peace and tranquility were food for my soul, and I couldn't get enough of it. Even at some of my sickest moments, I would picture myself underwater—at total peace and away from the illnesses that were trying to drown me. I could always go into a peaceful meditative state when I was underwater.

But I've become terrified of real water.

You're doing so good, Victoria.

You're back in the water.

Just relax.

Go back to your peaceful place.

I hold on for dear life as my brother Will holds me and moves me around in the water. Both Will and Cam are so supportive, and they cheer me as I struggle to swim. The life jacket is snug, and it continually tugs at my feeding tube, which is a source of discomfort to begin with. I am uncomfortable and frustrated. I feel constricted and confused.

How can I ever swim again?

I can barely move my arms, and my legs don't work.

The girl who could fly through the water can barely float on her own.

Nothing will ever be the same.

My brothers are persistent, and day after day, they take me to the pool and swim with me. Eventually, I hold on to my brothers less and find movement and fluidity in the water. It's not easy, but I am now determined. My illnesses and horrible experiences have already taken so much from me, and I am not going to let the water be added to the list.

The whole summer of 2010—before I start high school (cue the scary music)—is dedicated to me regaining me. I want my life back. And although my life is different than it was, this is still *my* life. Water was one of the biggest parts of my life before all of this, and my brothers know that.

But then, another goal pushes to the surface—school. This is definitely on the back burner of my mind.

Will I be able to go back to school?

What will the kids think of me?

Will I be able to make up all the time that I've lost?

I've always been a strong student, and I try to remind myself of that daily. But the reality is that I have not been in school since the fifth grade, and now, just before my sixteenth birthday, I am supposed to go to high school—*high school!* Will and Cam are sophomores, and I want to catch up to them. Recently my family moved to Exeter, New Hampshire. My mum grew up there, and they have a fantastic school system. It's funny, but ever since I was little, and my family would visit Exeter, it always felt like home to me. But now, I am the new kid in school—and that's never fun.

Especially if you're the new kid, in a wheelchair, with a feeding tube, crooked teeth, bangs, and a double chin. Let's just say, my first day of school is far from stellar.

Some of the kids are cruel, and they make sure I know that I do *not* belong and that I am "different." As if I don't already know that. I am mocked daily for the mere fact that I am in a wheelchair. Nobody gives me the time of day or talks to me, except my brothers and occasionally my cousins who are in a grade above me. I feel so lost and confused, and this makes me even more upset with my situation and being wheelchair-bound. I never actually felt different and like I didn't belong until I go to school.

And to top it off, I am put in a class where we color. Yes, *color*. It is a "special" class. I don't need to color; I want to learn. But when I was tested back in the summer, I was still significantly compromised. Reading is still making its way back into my life, among other basic skills. And my case manager is a real pain in the bum bum and won't listen to me or what my goals are. So, being the feisty now-sixteen-year-old who doesn't have time for those who don't believe in me, I go directly to the guidance counselor and demand that I be put in college-prep, "normal" classes, because I want to have a career and I want to go to college. My body may have been taken away from me, but my brain is very much alive and healthy and ready to be inspired and taught. I set a very lofty goal of graduating with my brothers, which means I have to make up five years of school in three years. I am not going to be left behind or watch from the sidelines anymore.

Bring. It. On.

With the help of my mum and an incredible new case manager and an amazing guidance counselor, I set my course. It isn't easy, but I prove the doubters wrong. I'm given a "trial period," which, depending on how my first semester goes, will determine if I can continue down this "crazy" path. At the end of my first semester, my report card is filled with As and Bs, which not only blows away my teachers, but also quiets the doubters who were so quick to judge and discourage my goals. I am on the right track and finally in the groove.

But I still struggle with the social part. I have not interacted in a "normal" setting since I was eleven. Needless to say, I am *not* eleven now, and I have much to learn about the social aspect of things. The world is very different, and high school feels like a foreign country. The kids my age say things and act in ways I truly do not understand. I mostly keep to myself and try to stay away from the halls when other kids are there, because I don't want to be humiliated or laughed at, which is common wherever I go. My new case manager lets me escape to her office to get my work done. I ask for extra time to get to class so I can hide in her office until the halls are clear and all the kids are in class.

At school I'm very isolated, mostly because I'm so weary of the humiliation I feel when I'm around my classmates. I find solitude in my studies and focus my attention on them. I do what I can to avoid the mocking and staring and straight-out rudeness. I can't even go to the library without kids laughing and pointing. In some ways, I see why I am a target, with the wheelchair and feeding tube. But I don't see how that is an excuse for unkindness and mocking. If they only knew what I have been through and that it hasn't even been a year since I began to "wake up." If they understood, I don't think they would be so cruel.

But dealing with their unkindness only makes me stronger, and every day when I come home, Mummy builds me up and tells me how smart, beautiful, and strong I am. Kind of like Aibileen in *The Help* tells the little girl she takes care of: "You is kind, you is smart, you is important." My mum is a modern-day Aibileen. And she continually reminds me that "it's not about the quantity of friends you have but about the quality of friends you have." I never forget that.

When I got sick, a lot of my friends from the town I grew up in forgot about me. They were young, and I was so sick for so long. Their lives moved on—as they should. At the beginning, some friends did come to visit, but my appearance was upsetting, and I was often too ill for visitors. Also, my mummy was very protective of my dignity, so she did not allow many visitors.

I went from having a bucketful of friends down to just four solid friends. These four (Kendra, Sarah, Nicole, and Ben) stuck with me through it all. Kendra, whom I've been friends with since

I was five, sent me a card almost every week and she sent little gifts and posters. Ben, who has been my bestie since three, would visit no matter what state I was in. He was there for me and loved me. His mom, Karen, even bought school supplies for my brothers while I was away at the hospital, so Mum could check that task off her long to-do list. Sarah and Nicole were my two dearest friends from the swim team I was on before I got sick. We always went to swim meets together, and we'd do arts and crafts. All four of these friends stood by me throughout my journey and continued to be there for me as I recovered and made my way back into life. While Sarah and Nicole are at Exeter High School with me, Ben and Kendra are at another high school in the town we moved from. But they make a point to visit me often.

And then there is one other friend I am so thankful for: my dear friend Connor was the first friend I made post–vegetative state and while in a wheelchair. We met the day of the school winter carnival. I was sitting alone as usual, and he sat next to me. Instantly we became friends. It was so wonderful to have someone in high school (in addition to Sarah and Nicole) who didn't make fun of me and actually gave me the time of day. Connor is amazing and is the definition of a true friend.

After meeting Connor, it is great to know that not all kids are unkind and that I can make friends despite my wheelchair. When I think about it, I see that there are advantages to being left out. High school is filled with so much drama, and the more friends you have, the more drama you have. I'm thankful I have a handful of dear friends—and that's enough.

Besides, I have other plans that don't involve a super-successful high school social life. I couldn't care less that I'm not invited to parties or included in social events. I have bigger goals and things I want to achieve. I find my refuge elsewhere: *sports*.

Not long after that day my brothers throw me into the water, my arms start regaining movement and strength; although the progression is slow, I start to become more comfortable and at home with the water again. Before school started in September, I decided to ditch the life jacket. At first, I sink, because I've always relied on my legs to keep me upright. But once I start using my arms, I don't even notice that I can't use my legs. Being in the water and using my arms becomes normal and fluid and peaceful for me. I can unhook my feeding tube and escape my wheelchair. I know my feeding tube and wheelchair are crucial to my survival and my independence, but they also disrupt my inner peace. They get in the way of me feeling "normal" and free. The hour or so that I am swimming, I feel somewhat "normal." This is important to me, because at school I feel like such an outsider. But in the water, I *belong*.

And being in the water ignites something on the inside that has not been ignited in a long time.

Once an athlete, always an athlete.

Being an athlete and being incredibly competitive serve me

well in my rehabilitation. I channel all I know about being an athlete into surviving and learning to live and function again. But as I progress with my swimming, I start to feel that itch to compete. Getting into competition sounds like a preposterous idea in my head, but in my *heart*, I know I can do it. And Tom, my hockey coach, encourages me to take that leap. I had started hockey in the fall of this year and was loving every moment of it, continuing to reaffirm to my coach that I wanted to pursue hockey, not swimming. I think mainly because it was going to be so different than I remembered. Being a breaststroker before I got sick, I knew deep down that not being able to kick would prevent me from swimming like I did before. Kind of protecting my heart and starting a new page, staying away from things that reminded me of what was taken away from me. Sled hockey was different than stand-up hockey. It was still hockey, but it didn't make me feel like I needed my legs or missed them. But swimming, that was a whole different story. I missed my legs constantly. But sometimes you have to push through the pain and the things that remind you of what you lost to gain something even better. So, I kept swimming. I decided to just "go for it."

I've got nothing to lose and everything to gain.

I manage to get in touch with a coach who had coached my old swim team before I got sick. I begin training and practicing with his team. Before I know it, I am in my first competition in nearly five years.

"Take your mark."

BEEP!

Although I am beat by eight-year-olds, I don't care. I am back to doing what I love—competitive swimming. It's not easy, but little by little, I become faster and faster and more in tune with the water. But now that I'm swimming again, I realize that I've never truly appreciated my legs. I have always been a breaststroker, and not being able to kick makes every stroke—except for freestyle—nearly impossible. Nonetheless, I keep moving forward.

Just keep swimming.

Swimming once again becomes my refuge. The world around me seems chaotic and uncertain, but once I get in the water, I can forget it all. I forget the torment of school and the doubters and the hurdles. When I'm swimming, it's just me and the water, nothing else matters. I have no idea where swimming will take me, I just know that I need to get in the water every day. In many ways, swimming saves me and gives me a place where I belong. Something I had longed for and wished for since I came back.

As my swimming progresses, my life and my recovery progress as well. I am stronger and more independent, and I can actually maneuver a small, lightweight wheelchair, which makes all the difference. And because my tummy has miraculously healed, I no longer need my feeding tube and can finally eat and digest food normally. For nearly five years, I could not eat—for many reasons—but one of the main reasons was that my tummy completely shut down after the injury my spinal cord sustained from the TM. As a result, I had to be on a twenty-four-hour feeding-tube pump connected directly to my lower intestine. I have been able to keep it secret from most of my friends, but now I'm so excited to have it gone and to eat real food. Another check in the normalcy box!

For the first time in nearly five years, I'm feeling less like a patient and more like a human. I've jumped into school, and I'm redirecting the frustration of kids being cruel into catching up and graduating on time. I know that graduating with my triplet brothers will not be easy, but I believe it will be worth it. I'm playing sled hockey and traveling the country with my daddy, and I'm back in the water.

Finding my way back.

I want to compete, and I want to be fast, and I no longer want to do this only "for fun." So, my next hurdle is finding a swim team I can swim on and events to compete in. The team that I was training with was not a good fit for me and I needed to be challenged. My high school team won't give me a chance to compete on varsity, even though I have the times needed. And the swim clubs I am trying out with don't take me seriously. I am the "pity" swimmer in a wheelchair, and many judge me before they know me or my times. I spend most of the time at the pool with my mummy, who continues to encourage me and cheer me on.

I decide to reach out to my sled hockey coach, Tom Carr, and ask him where I can go with swimming.

His answer surprises me: "How about the Paralympics?" I know that sled hockey is a part of the winter Paralympics, but I didn't know a summer Paralympics even existed.

You mean I can compete with other athletes who can't kick, like me?

I begin my research and discover that the summer Games are just a year away, and they will be held in London! My mummy is from the UK, and a majority of my extended family live there. What a reunion and adventure it would be to go there. I've always wanted to go. So, I set my mind to going to London and representing my country. A lofty goal, given I have just gotten back into swimming, but I am ready for the challenge. I begin creating workouts and swimming with various teams, but I haven't yet found a coach who is the right fit. After all, I need someone who believes in achieving the impossible because this seems impossible.

In the meantime, my family bands together to support my "impossible" dream in the best ways they can. My uncle Russ takes me out to the lake every morning, parks the boat, and floats in the water as a marker for me to train. Each lap he cheers for me.

I finally find a great coach named Nicole with the help of my mummy, and before I know it, we are heading out to my first Paralympic-style meet in western Massachusetts. I am shocked to see people like me, in wheelchairs and dealing with various disabilities, competing in actual events. The meet is fantastic—better than expected—and I am on cloud nine.

Shortly after the meet, I am greeted by the meet director. He is so excited and happy about how I raced. "What are your plans with swimming?"

"I want to go to the London 2012 Paralympics next year."

I will never forget the bewildered look on his face. "Next year?" he asks.

"Yes."

He is at a loss for words and struggles to find the right thing to say. I just stare at him and smile—I don't see what's so confusing. After about a minute, he kneels down, puts his hand on my shoulder, half-smiles, and says, "Sweetie, you don't stand a chance. Athletes have been training for years to make it to the Games next year. I really don't think that should be your goal. Maybe you'll have a chance in the next four years at the next summer Games."

What?

I am crushed, but all I can think in my head is,

Don't 'sweetie' me, sir.

I politely smile and leave the pool. I can't get out of there soon enough! How could someone be so bluntly cruel and just smash a dream without giving any sense of hope or optimism? If my journey has taught me nothing else, it's taught me the power of hope and optimism. We really don't know what we're capable of until we try—and either fail or fly. But you'll never know until you actually take that leap and go for it and try. I've always believed that when you take that leap of faith you'll either be given the wings to fly or God will catch you.

I don't say much on the car ride home with my mom; I just keep my head down and ponder what that man said.

Was he right?

Is this a crazy goal?

What if I fail?

I don't want to make a fool of myself.

I guess I really don't know if I can do it.

He's been in the Paralympic world, so he probably knows best.

As I ponder my thoughts, I begin to doubt my swimming dreams and goals. I am beyond devastated and can't hide it. One thing about my mummy is that she knows me better than anybody else. Sure, that's how most moms are, but after what we've gone through together, it's a knowing on a whole different level.

Mummy isn't saying much, and I can tell that something's not right with her. She abruptly pulls into a Dunkin' Donuts parking lot and turns to me with a passionate, fearless stare and a pointed index finger. In her most intense voice, she says, "Don't you ever let someone tell you what you can or can't do. If you believe it and work hard for it, you can achieve anything. And don't let anyone ever tell you different! You've come too far and overcome too much to let some person tell you what you cannot achieve."

In an instant, my heart is filled, and the fire is ignited. My mom is right (she always is): who is this person to tell me what I could and couldn't do? He doesn't know me or what I'm capable of. One thing about me—when you tell me I can't do something,

I become determined to prove you wrong. And one thing about Mummy—she never backs down from a challenge. I definitely get that from her.

And so it begins.

That man's words become fuel for me to swim faster and stronger. In September of 2011, I travel to my first official Paralympic swim meet in Santa Clara, California. To say I feel intimidated is an understatement. I am the new kid in a very experienced and veteran world. All the swimmers around me have on their special race suits and their USA caps, and they know what they are doing. I do not. I'm just the rookie from New Hampshire. The London 2012 Paralympic Games are just a year away.

The pressure is on.

All I need to do is swim fast and see where that takes me.

Well . . . not only do I swim fast, but I manage to break an American record, qualify for the Paralympic trials, and become a member of the national team. This is a lot to take in, given the fact that just a month prior, I had been told to not even try. Many coaches and swimmers are baffled. "Who is this kid from New Hampshire?" I had come out of nowhere, and I am starting to make waves, literally and figuratively.

This is only the beginning.

In swimming, it's all about qualifying for various meets and getting faster. I'm traveling to meets, but even though I broke a record, I'm not improving much on my times. My times are decent, but nowhere close to qualifying for the Paralympics. I know I need something more, but I don't know where to start.

Coach Tom recommends that I meet with a coach down in Beverly, Massachusetts, named John Ogden. I am incredibly thankful for my former coach's help, but I need to step up my training and train in long-course meters, something my current coach isn't able to help me with. The Beverly YMCA has a renowned swimming program, and when I arrive at the facility, I know immediately that this is the place. Coach John is tough, and he meets me with a stern handshake. We go into a meeting room, and he gets right to it. "What are your goals?" he asks sternly.

"I want to make the USA Paralympic swimming team and go to London."

"You want to make the team and compete at the Games in six months?"

"Yes."

I was honestly so used to seeing bewildered looks from coaches in the past that I expect John to deliver the same look. To my surprise he smiles and asks me . . .

"How about winning a gold medal?"

As soon as he says this, I can't help but laugh out loud. I look over at my mom and shake my head.

"That would be amazing, but I know that is not possible."

"Why not? Who says so?" John continues to stare sternly at me. His eyes are focused and piercing. I know right then and there that he isn't kidding. He is serious. Never in my life have I seen someone so sure and so confident, not even cracking the slightest of smiles.

"Wait, are you serious?"

"Of course I am—if I'm going to train you, that will be the goal."

I am shocked and pleased. For the first time ever, a coach believes in me and has even bigger goals than I do. John sees something even I don't see.

"It's not going to be easy, and we are going to have to work really hard. None of this half-a** stuff; you have to promise me that you're all in. Seven days a week, two to three hours a day. This will be your job; aside from school, this needs to be your focus. So, are you in?"

"I'm in."

I promise.

I soon learn that I had no idea what I was signing up for. Before I know it, I go from swimming 1,500 to 2,000 yards (on a good day) to 8,000 to 10,000 yards. Never in my life have I been pushed so hard and challenged. I am swimming with elite swimmers who are committed to Division one schools and training for the Olympic trials.

One of the biggest differences about this place is that I am treated like everyone else. At school, my peers look down on me, but here I am an equal. My fellow swimmers talk to me and don't just see my wheelchair. They treat me like the normal human I am. If I need help, they are there to help me, and when my coach makes me stay for an extra forty minutes after a grueling two-hour practice, they cheer for me and root me on as I get my butt kicked.

My time at this pool is not only motivating; it is healing, and it restores my faith in kids my age. I have a place where I belong; I am respected and treated equally, and after what I have been through, that is much needed and desired.

Not long into my training, I start to see results. Coach John pushes me further and further each week, and there are many times I don't know how I am going to get out of the pool and wheel myself to the locker room. My arms are complete Jell-O, but I love it. I haven't ever pushed myself this hard in my entire life. One thing about me is that I love a good challenge and I love to be pushed.

Getting my driver's license is not part of the equation yet, so Mummy—once again being the amazing human she is—makes the two-hour round-trip, seven days a week, rain or shine. We often get punchy during the 3:00 a.m. commutes and precarious-weather trips. I am so tired that one morning, I actually open the sunroof instead of turning on the overhead light, allowing a significant amount of snow to pour into the car. And despite the two-hour car ride, if I am even a minute or two late, John sprays me with a cold hose as I make my way onto the pool deck and into the water. And sometimes, if I don't go fast enough, he'll do the same because he "feels like it will motivate me." Although it isn't always pleasant to get sprayed, it is nice to have my coach treat me like all of his other swimmers and not like the "special" wheelchair kid. And that cold hose definitely made me swim faster.

My swimming mentality begins to change: being surrounded by so many elite athletes, I am more determined than ever to swim really fast. At first, my goal is not to get lapped, but that goal quickly becomes "get to the front of the lane and keep up." Coach John pushes me to limits I don't know I am capable of. And he sees something in me that I still don't quite yet see. When I question why I have to do these crazy drills and stay for extra practice, John says, "You want to win gold?"

"Yes."

"Well, all of those other swimmers have been training a lot longer than you; we must not only catch up, we need to be better, faster, and stronger." He reminds me of this every day and every moment I think I can't go any further. But this really is my kind of catch-up. The loss of all those years has become the motivation—though sometimes borderline insanity—for me to train like crazy. My hard work pays off at the next meet.

"What is she doing here?" I hear a girl who is around my age say to her mother. Her mother then looks at me and my wheelchair and rolls her eyes.

It is the final of the 800-meter freestyle, and since this is a timed final and we're swimming in a massive pool, we will be splitting the lanes which means that two swimmers will swim next to each other splitting up the lane. It's pretty common for this to happen with local meets and with the longer distance events. I have never swum the 800, but my coach is optimistic that I can do well, given that most distance swimmers don't use their legs much. Distance swimming is all about endurance, timing out your speed and energy, and finding the right momentum. It's also about remaining calm, cool, and collected.

My daddy is with me, and being a hockey guy, he knows *nothing* about swimming. All he knows is that he has to press the red button on the stopwatch to get my time. During longer races at local meets oftentimes parents or swimmers help with the timing. This is a first for my daddy. "Good luck, sweetie." He pats my back and steps next to the mother of the swimmer I'll be sharing the lane with—the same swimmer who made the rude remark about me. She takes off. Twenty seconds later, it's my turn.

"Take your mark . . ."

BEEP!

Swimming, especially distance swimming, is always a very calming experience for me. I love having the time to inch my way slowly but surely up. Distance is all mental, and you have to get yourself into somewhat of a meditative state and keep your mind and body relaxed. The key is to trust your training, always.

Just keep swimming.

As the event goes on, I see Coach John on the side of the pool signaling me to go a little faster with each lap. Trusting my training and realizing that this is *nothing* compared to what I swim on a daily basis, I oblige. As I follow his signals, I start to see the kicking feet of my lane buddy. She is running out of steam, and we still have about halfway to go. Being a bit sassy, I turn up the speed.

"What is she doing here?"

I play the words over and over again in my head, like gasoline fueling me to catch her.

John begins to jump up and down excitedly, as I pass my lane partner. I can hear my teammates freaking out, and I can see John waving his arms up and down. At this point, I have about two hundred to go and decide to sprint the rest. My arms fly, and I can feel my body literally being lifted out of the water. That is when I know . . .

I can go far.

I can win.

I can beat her.

I'll never forget the moment I lapped that girl and touched the wall. I am so excited about lapping her that I don't even realize my time. My daddy—being the naïve "hockey guy turned swimming timer"—pats me on the head and says, "Good job, sweetie." I could've had the worst race of my life, and he'd still be proud. That is just who he is and who my parents are. They never pressure us or act like those "sport" parents who live vicariously through their children. They just want us to be happy and have fun. Dad winks at me and directs my eyes to the girl's mother, who sits baffled that

I have beaten her daughter. That woman is *not* happy. I am relishing that moment when my coach starts to scream, "World record, world record! She broke the world record!"

World record?

I had been made vaguely aware of the record, but I had no expectations of breaking it. After all, I have never swum the freestyle 800 competitively, so I am just getting my feet wet. Breaking a world record has never actually felt attainable. Growing up I have been obsessed with *The Guinness Book of World Records,* but I never thought that I would one day achieve a world record. Until I started training with John, I'd never even focused on times; I had just been trying to get to the other end of the pool in one piece.

You can do this.

Everything changes after that moment. Even though the 800 is not a Paralympic event in London, it still sets the stage and the expectation for the trials. The momentum and fire I felt from that race ignites a spark that my coach has been trying so hard to get hold of. I am swimming fast—fastest in the world—and I like that feeling. Who wouldn't? After I break that first world record, I want to keep breaking them. This becomes my all-consuming focus. I want to keep being the fastest. Like a race car driver, I want to keep going and beating everyone else.

Faster.

Faster.

Faster.

I break several of the American and Pan-American records, and I start inching my way closer to several world records, which puts me in medal contention for the Games. I have broken the distance world records, but those events are not in the Games. Only the 400, 100, and 50 freestyle will be events in London, and these are what I'm aiming to compete in.

Coach John is my rock, and at meets it feels like it is just me and him. I don't know many of the national team members yet, and being the outsider, I'm not always welcomed warmly. But I am used to doing my own thing, and as long as John is by my side, I am good. We have a system and a mind-set going into every practice and meet. We are a team, and our focus is plain and simple.

Go for gold.

But in the back of my mind, I truly just want to make the US Paralympic team. Anything after that will be icing on the cake. Nonetheless, John keeps pushing me and motivating me to go faster and be greater. Through the grueling practices and various meets, with little time to rest, we develop a momentum that sets out a pretty clear golden path. We are trying to achieve the "impossible," with just under six months' training time left, and that is at times incredibly stressful for John and for me. But little by little, it seems less impossible, and John won't let me slow down. It is all or nothing. Although, it took him a little while to understand my quirks and superstitions . . .

I have always been a very superstitious person when it comes to sports and my routine. Since I was little, I had my swim routine down to a science. Same type of PowerBar, blue Gatorade, goggles, cap, and swimsuit. I also have a very "interesting" way in which I prep for an event I am swimming. Between my superstitions and mental preparedness approach, I think John thought I was nuts. And what I do right before a race probably sealed the deal on me being nuts.

"So, this is the one hundred free?" I ask John. "I move my arms like this?" (Doing the freestyle motion.)

"You're kidding me, right?" The look he gives me is a mixture of confusion, worry, and concern. What John hasn't realized yet is that this is how I work and how I prepare. But after that first world record, John realizes that whatever quirks and superstitions I have, they work really well for me. So instead of questioning me or looking at me puzzled, he just smiles, shakes his head, and pats my cap. "Just swim fast, kid. Trust your training."

Most of the meets we attend (aside from the required Paralympic meets) are able-bodied meets, which means I am the only person in a wheelchair and without the use of my legs. I am no longer getting crushed by eight-year-olds, and I am keeping up with the best of them. I'm not coming in first, but I'm never last, and that's all that matters to me.

Just don't be last.

It's crazy writing and saying that I just don't want to be last, but I've spent so much time behind that I appreciate even being second-to-last. It's a sign that I am getting stronger and getting faster.

However, I know that one of these days, I'm going to be first. I am determined. But you can't truly appreciate being first without coming in last over and over again. It's humbling, maddening, and frustrating to be last. But it only makes coming in first all the more amazing and exciting.

9

FROM BREAKING RECORDS
TO NEAR DEFEAT

June 2012 to September 2012

"A new world record has been set!" The crowd screams as I emerge from the water. Since coming back into the world, I'm not a fan of loud noises and huge crowds. I look around and try to get my bearings. I hear something being announced about a world record. Trying to shift my focus from the race I just swam, I lean over to the swimmer next to me and ask, "No way, who broke the world record? That's so cool."

"You did," she says matter-of-factly. "Congrats."

Wait, me?

I did it?

In front of all these people?

It's day one of the London 2012 Paralympic swimming trials,

and I am swimming the 400 freestyle. Just a few months ago (before I started to train with John), I thought of this race as a cooldown, and I didn't really know how to swim it. In fact, I didn't know how to do sprint work in general.

Because I don't have the horsepower of my legs, sprint work is *so* much harder for me than distance swimming. My arms like to go one speed and trying to make them go faster is incredibly challenging. Distance (once I figured it out) came easy to me—even when competing in able-bodied events. You do not necessarily need your legs to be good at distance swimming.

But when I'm told I've broken the world record, all I feel is shock. I needed to do well in this event so I would be in good contention to make the US team. I was not rested for this meet, and leading up to it, I was pretty beat up from practice. But because I trust John and his coaching and training, I do what I always do—get to the wall fast.

Coach John is going to be so proud.

I swim over to the side of the pool where John is waiting with my wheelchair. I am expecting a little compliment from him, but in true John fashion all he says is, "You could've gone faster." And this is the closest thing to a compliment I get from John that day. I have gone faster than anyone in the world, and yet Coach John wants more. This is part of what makes him a great coach versus a good coach. Even after reaching the "best in the world" in this event, John reminds me that I can always reach higher.

Many people are satisfied when they break a record or reach a specific goal (and there's nothing wrong with that), but my goals and John's goals and visions are beyond what I can do at any given moment. He and I believe that I should never stop being challenged and setting goals. There's nothing wrong with celebrating and enjoying, but you've got to keep climbing and stay hungry.

Stay hungry.

Swim faster.

Eyes on the prize.

Later in the meet, I break an additional world record in the 400 free, and I break American and Pan-American records in the 50 freestyle and 100 breaststroke.

But John keeps saying the same thing, "You could've gone faster." And I do go faster with each race, but we never stop pushing. I haven't yet qualified for the team, so I can't sit back and relish my victory, assuming I will make the team. In fact, I am nervous and worried that I *won't* make the team. Even after breaking three records, I refuse to believe that I have made the team until my name is announced.

John and I focus on every meet and race as it comes up. For the first time in my life, I am ahead, but I swim and train like I am behind. "Don't focus on making the team," John says. "Just race and go fast. That is all I want you to do. The rest will come." One race after another, faster times, breaking records and earning respect.

"Victoria Arlen, welcome to the two thousand twelve US Paralympic Swim Team!"

That's me!

My name, me, the girl who was told just three years ago that she'll never amount to anything is named to the US Paralympic Swim Team.

I did it.

I'm going to London.

• • •

At the time trials, I sit in an auditorium in the middle of Bismarck, North Dakota, and wait as they continue to call out the swimmers' names. I'm grasping the backpack in my lap that says, "Team USA, 2012." Several names are called, and many are not. I watch as swimmers who have trained so hard and so long leave in tears while others jump for joy. My heart breaks for the swimmers who did not make the team.

The auditorium is filled with a mixture of emotions. I feel bad for the swimmers who didn't make the team. I have come to know quite a few of them throughout the meets, and they deserve a chance, too. But that's just not how it works. You have to swim fast, and if you don't, then that's it. Swimming can be a cutthroat sport, and if you do well, your heart is full, and if you don't do as well, you can be heartbroken.

The team is escorted out of the auditorium and into meetings. I get to briefly hug my mummy and thank her, as tears run down her face. John has left for another meet, but I text him with the news. I should have known what he'd say: "Great. Time to get back to work. Need to get faster."

Holy moly.

I'm going to London.

In the meetings, we are each handed folders with paragraph after paragraph of team rules, flag and anthem etiquette, and Olympic and Paralympic history. This is real; I'm not dreaming! I don't realize at the time that there's a media firestorm going on outside.

As soon as I touch down in Boston, my phone begins to ring. Major news networks are calling and requesting my time for interviews. With headlines such as "Swimmer from New Hampshire Breaks Swimming Star Ellie Simmonds's Record" and "It Will Be the Battle of the Teenagers in London."

All of a sudden, I have to start dealing with the media. This is the first time I've been asked to share my story . . .

I don't want to share my story.

I'm not a fan of hoopla and people making a big deal. I just like to do my thing and make my family and God proud. I don't like showboating or boasting. This journey has cemented a humbleness within me. But the "media" world is relentless about my story. And I know that as soon as I share details, they won't leave me alone. So, I keep my story as vague as I can and try to brush over the whole vegetative state/unresponsive period of my life. I want to keep the story about swimming and London. But they keep digging, and before I know it, I am an "international inspiration." Balancing media appearances and training is incredibly difficult and leaves little to no time for "fun." It is work, work, and more work. And if I don't work "hard enough" for John's standards, I get extra work.

On top of that, I soon discover that there is another firestorm going on behind the scenes. Not only did I break Ellie's records, but I awoke a dragon overseas.

In the Paralympics, each participant must be "classified" by the International Paralympic Committee (IPC) before they can compete in any Paralympic-sanctioned meet. For swimmers, a classification session consists of a bench test and a swim test. During the bench test, they check out your body using a point system that ranks your abilities. They go through every limb and muscle group and extensively test it. Then they calculate the numbers.

Then comes the swim test, which has a whole separate point system for your swimming. After that, they watch a race and make their final classification conclusion. With every classification appointment, I was an S6 across the board. The S indicates the event (freestyle, butterfly, and backstroke) and the classes range from 1 (most impaired) to 10 (least impaired).

But a couple of individuals are not convinced of my classification since I broke two world records at trials. So, I receive an email stating that my classification is being "questioned." When I was seventy-fifth in the world, no one questioned my classification, but as soon as I am number one, everything changes.

Apparently, people in the past have faked being disabled so they could go to the Games. When I first heard that, I couldn't help but laugh.

You'd have to be pretty messed up in the head to do that.
Trust me, if I had a choice, I would NOT want to be disabled.
I hate being in a wheelchair.

Because this is an Olympic year and because I virtually came out of nowhere, they are suspicious. Understandably so, but they don't realize that during the last six years I have been fighting for my life; coming out of a vegetative state; learning how to move, eat, and function normally; and learning how to swim using just my arms.

I'm not "secretly" plotting to fake my way to the Paralympics. Nonetheless, I have to gather a significant amount of documentation to verify my disability and be reevaluated at the Games. I am devastated. I just want to focus on my training and plan out my competition schedule. My family is buying tickets and making plans to come to the Games. If I am moved into a different classification, my whole schedule would be thrown off and my family couldn't watch me. We have quite the crew going over to London, and I don't want them to miss my races.

But Coach John doesn't let it derail me. "Channel this into your training. Regardless of what they do or say, we will be ready. You will be ready." As hard as Coach John is on me, I understand that he knows what I am capable of, and he wants to help me get into a "better, stronger, and faster" mind-set. Sometimes he and I are like oil and water. He pushes me sometimes close to the edge. And he knows the right things to say to piss me off, and it always gets me to go faster. He knows my potential and expects excellence every minute that we train. If I'm not breaking records in practice or coming close to breaking them, there are consequences and harder sets. And the occasional cold hose spraying me. Sometimes after a two-hour practice I stay behind and have "impossible" times I have to make. If I don't make the times John sets for me, then I keep going and going and going until I make the times. Sometimes practices are over three hours. As much as I'm tired and at times frustrated, I secretly love training this way. But John is always the voice of reason. Each meet, I get faster and more confident in my abilities. I am on a crash course for the international stage.

Eat.

Breathe.

Swim.

Sleep.

Over and over again.

Until . . . time to go.

Before I know it, I am on a flight to Germany to begin training camp. I have become friends with most of the swimmers, and we very quickly become a family. I have never been overseas or traveled such a distance in my wheelchair. I honestly have no expectations other than to enjoy this adventure. I have yet to master the art of sleeping on an airplane, so by the time we touch down in Stuttgart, I have been up for almost twenty-four hours. Deliriously tired, we arrive at the US army base and are introduced to our "host families," who are various military families that live on the base.

I am blessed to be paired with an incredible family who take me to downtown Stuttgart and to church. They give me that family feeling that I am desperately missing. My host family is a blessing from God. They show me the country and allow me to feel less homesick.

Because I have to be reevaluated, I—along with a few other swimmers—have to leave Germany and go to London. We are very disappointed, because we miss out on the US team arrival festivities.

Two of the top classifiers are assigned to classify me, and my meeting with them is bright and early in the morning. They have been given page after page of documentation, which confirms my spinal cord injury from TM and details my various upper-body impairments, including the spasticity in my hands and arms—which is still present and causing me issues.

The evaluation room is underneath the stands of the pool and has concrete white walls and no windows. I am with my Team USA liaison Erin, whom I initially met when I was classified a year ago. The experts walk in, look at my hands—which of course, are spastic—and walk out. For two more hours, Erin and I wait and wait and wait. Nobody enters the room.

"What's going on?"

"I'm not sure," Erin says with a concerned look. "This shouldn't be taking so long." In my experience this past year, classification appointments are usually less than an hour from start to finish.

Knock, knock.

The classifiers finally reenter the room and walk toward Erin and me. I immediately get a sick feeling in my stomach. At first, they look at each other and then at Erin, but they don't look me in the eye. And then they say the words I will *never* forget.

"Clearly, you're disabled, but we cannot classify you."

"What?"

My heart sinks. I know at that very moment that this is about way more than my classification. Tears run down my face uncontrollably; the classifiers look down and still don't make eye contact. They nod their heads and walk out. Erin chases after them, demanding an explanation, but they refuse. Julie (another classifier expert with Team USA) rushes in and asks what's wrong. Erin explains, and Julie immediately leaves to speak with the classifiers. I am numb, absolutely numb, and the next few minutes are a complete blur. Erin wheels me into the locker room, and I fall into her arms, crying.

"Why is this happening? What did I do wrong? This makes no sense."

"This is not right, Victoria, and we are going to get to the bottom of this." We both know that this is beyond wrong, but it is out of our hands. The classifiers had refused to give us an explanation, and so we just pray that there will be answers. In any kind of crisis or problem, I'm okay when I know why and how. I'm not okay when there is no explanation or reason. We are in the blind. I manage to call my parents, who have just touched down in London, and I can barely talk.

"They won't let me swim."

"Why?"

"I, I, I, don't know."

Click.

I hang up the call, and my phone slips from my hands. I've been through so much, I have beaten the odds thrown against me, and now these two experts who won't even look me in the eye refuse to do their jobs and classify me, and they refuse to offer an explanation.

Fortunately, the US delegation is all over it. Julie is a strong-willed and determined woman, and she does *not* stand for injustice. Lawyers are brought in, and the fight begins. I am numb. The rest of the US team arrived earlier that afternoon, and they quickly learn of the news. I don't want to talk to anyone; I just want to be alone. My coaches bring my parents into the village, and all I can do is cry, cry, and cry. My heart is cut in half and blown into smithereens. I am absolutely heartbroken.

I had dreamed of this moment and of being here representing my country on a world stage . . . *the* world stage. And yet, here I sit in a locker room bathroom, gutted, confused, and beyond upset. When my parents call me back, I can't even speak to them.

This is humiliating.

I have done nothing wrong.

I think about the time when I was little and was asked what I wanted to be when I grew up. All I could think of was a shiny gold medal, like the one my swimming idol, Jenny Thompson, won at the Olympics. I remember a picture I had drawn then. I had a sparkly medal around my neck and a smile that was far too big for the stick figure. I think about little Victoria who *idolized* the Olympics and dreamed of the day she'd be here. This pool, the village, the Team USA swag, and the chance to go for gold. I thought that this would be my dream coming true, that the past two years of fighting back from the pain and the vegetative state would all pay off here. But instead of a dream come true, I'm living in a horrible nightmare. And the worst thing about it is that I hadn't done anything to deserve this, except work hard and swim fast. Which is kind of what you're supposed to do to get to this level. I worked my butt off to get here and now . . . for what?

Was it over?

Too good to be true?

It's not fair.

None of this is fair.

While my teammates enjoy the festivities of the village and prepare for opening ceremonies, I spiral into the despair of the unknown.

Will I be able to swim?

Will they send me home?

I don't want to let everyone down.

To top it off, the media catch wind of the "news" and have a field day. Everywhere I go, my face is spread across tabloids, news-papers, and television news shows. I refuse to comment or speak to anyone. I just want to be left alone.

Please leave me alone.

And so, I pray . . . and trust. It is out of my hands and in God's.

God, please.

I really, really, really need you.

In Germany during training camp, my friend and teammate Courtney and I started a prayer group. It turned out that there are quite a few strong men and women of God on our team. I learned a lot about the power of prayer, but even more about praying to-gether. Having a network of believers during one of the craziest times of my life is beyond a blessing.

When I finally leave that locker room and come back to the

village, Courtney is waiting with open arms, along with my friend and teammate Brad. The two of them sit with me, hug me, and provide the words of comfort and optimism that I need to hear. I try to keep things on the down-low. I usually keep a close-knit circle. Though we are like family, a few of my teammates are not big fans of mine. I had come out of nowhere, and I was young and fast. And to be honest, I don't want to give them any fuel for disliking me.

Hold it in.

Take a breath.

You're okay.

Bury the pain.

Just bury it.

It's what you do best.

"Do you want to go to the hotel and be with your family?" Queenie, who is the USA team manager, kindly asks.

"Thank you, Queenie, but no thanks."

I want to be here for my team and keep things as normal as possible for them. I love my roommates, and I don't want to throw them off their game. As much as I want to be with my family, I know I should stay. I've always tried to be a team player, so I'm not leaving now. Although, once my mummy arrives at the village, I spend much of my time curled up in the fetal position crying in her lap. I know that I need to stay here, despite my sadness.

I need to be here.

Though my world has come to a standstill, the Games are still in full swing. The joy, excitement, and pride of all the athletes from all the countries fill the air. Each athlete here has "made it," has achieved the dream, and is enjoying the event, as they should. They deserve it. I desperately want to share that joy, but each time I feel a hint of excitement, tears quickly follow.

I can't let my guard down.

So, I return to the coping method I've used so often in the past years. I go numb, no emotions, just blank. It's easier to take the pain when you're numb. Is it good to be numb? Probably not. Do I care at this moment? No, I don't really care about anything except justice, fairness, and being given a fair shot at swimming.

I just want to swim.

It's August 29, 2012, and opening ceremonies are under way. As I march with my team, tears are running down my face, but I do the best I can to put on a smile.

Be proud.

Put on your game face.

Tom, one of our team coaches, pushes my wheelchair through the stadium for the march. Tom is in my close circle: he believes in me and has prayed with me and for me. Tom, Courtney, and Brad remind me to keep trusting God and to stay strong.

Remember.

Terrible beginnings often have incredible endings.

After what seems like an eternity and a lot of sleepless nights and hard work from the US delegation, my case is presented to an appeals court. The USA team has gathered an immense amount of medical records and paperwork, all proving that I am eligible to swim. In addition to this overwhelming evidence and the fact that the classifiers did not abide by the rules in refusing to classify me, the British prime minister, David Cameron, actually makes a public statement, "This is about athleticism not politics," referring to the competition between Ellie and me. The politics are out of my control and are unfortunately a downside. But, after all this, an independent group of arbitrators rules in my favor and I am granted classification reevaluation.

Thank you, God.

I can now shift my focus, get classified, and prepare. Except for one little issue: the classifiers are nowhere to be found. After two more days, a classification appointment is scheduled on the eve of my first race: the 400 freestyle.

Julie accompanies me to the appointment, and right away we see that they are going around in circles. Thoughts race through my head.

This shouldn't be taking this long.

I already did that test.

It's been over two hours.

This isn't fair.

As previously mentioned, classification appointments are usually an hour at most. But almost four hours have passed. Julie is not happy, and I am exhausted. The classifiers are reviewing my medical records and recalculating the scores from the tests they've already conducted. I am asked to do additional tests I had never been required to do in previous classifications, and I am relentlessly questioned about my condition.

They stare at me and talk to me in a tone that indicates they think I'm hiding something. But there is nothing to hide. My medical records confirm my physical impairments. If anything, I am more impaired than they realize. I do a bench test, pool test, bench test again, and coordination test. One classifier even says, "I'm not sure why we are doing this; she is clearly disabled."

Please, just let me swim.

Please.

After what seems like an eternity of unnecessary questions, they conclude with, "You belong in the S6 category."

Without an apology for the insanely long and exhausting testing, they leave. To be honest, at this point I don't even care. I just want to compete.

10

SPLASH!

September 2012 to June 2013

"Take your mark . . ."

BEEP!

It's September 1, 2012, and more than twenty thousand spectators are in the crowd that day in London, with millions more from around the world tuned in. It is my first official day of competition, and I am swimming the 400-meter freestyle. As the current world record holder and the focus of all the classification drama, I am subject to lots of cameras in my face as I make my way to the starting block. The aquatic stadium booms with noise, and I nearly have a heart attack as I enter the pool. Everyone wants to see the "battle of the teenagers." I am terrified. And as I hit the water, I feel my entire body tremble uncontrollably.

You can do this, Victoria.

One stroke.

Two strokes.

Three strokes.

Breathe.

To keep my nerves at bay, I continue to count my strokes and tune out the audience. I have the lead, but I can tell that Ellie is coming up behind me. I quickly realize I have gone out way too fast due to a massive adrenaline rush. My arms are toast on the final fifty, and I am tapping into my reserve. Ellie is a little person, which means that she has complete use of both her arms and her legs, versus me having only the use of my arms. I never have understood how it is fair for us to compete against each other, but I guess the thought is that her short stature is somewhat similar to my not having use of my lower half.

I can hear the crowd getting louder and louder, and sure enough, Ellie has turned on her legs and is charging my way. I put my head down and continue to swim, but deep down I know that not having my legs to propel me on that last fifty is a major disadvantage.

Though Ellie wins the gold in this race, I am quite all right with my silver medal. I can't help but think about how just two years prior I was barely holding my head up and my brothers were holding me in the water. I could barely move and now I'm here with a shiny silver medal. And honestly, I'm pretty happy that I didn't poop my suit out of fear.

Wow.

This crowd, this pool, I'm here.

I made it.

Even with all I've been through, I feel like I'm glowing. It just doesn't get any better than winning a medal. I can feel myself starting to relax and actually enjoy the Games. I realize that this race had been more than a race for me. It was about another mountain I had to climb, and it was about overcoming the fear and anxiety that had been drilled into my head by the IPC drama and classification issues.

Finally, I could just swim.

The next few days are a blur of practicing, racing, and cheering my teammates on. I go on to receive two more silver medals in the 50 freestyle and 4 by 100 freestyle relay—an event that I find out on the day of the final that I will be competing in. I have not been in a relay since I was eleven years old, and starting from my bum on the blocks is a whole different ball game than being on my feet. Nonetheless, I dive in as the second leg of the relay, and I am the *only* swimmer who can't kick. I am a last-minute addition to the relay due to my fast times in my previous race. We haven't competed together before and we are up against some pretty fast swimmers from other countries. But despite the odds, we win silver and beat the UK, which is a major upset.

All seems well until my second-to-last race: the 100 breaststroke.

Something's not right.

Growing up primarily as a breaststroker, my coaches have always encouraged me to pursue and continue this stroke. It is beyond hard to feel the fluidity without kicking. But I keep working at it. My hard work pays off, and by the time I'm in London, I am second in the world in my classification for the 100-meter breaststroke. I am a medal contender for this event.

The pressure is on.

The woman in first place is nearly twice my age and is a "complete beast," meaning she had the record by almost a minute, and nobody came near her. I never felt super strong and confident in any breaststroke events, and the only reason aside from my coaches that I swim it, is that it is the first event I broke an American record in. It has a special place in my heart. On this particular day, I am not feeling right at all. I have been struggling with debilitating muscle spasms, and the breaststroke seems to induce them whenever I swim it. Most athletes know when they have it or do not have it. It's an instinct, a feeling when you just know you got this.

I don't got this.

As soon as I dive in, I know I don't have it. My body tenses up, and I find myself trying harder than ever to get to the wall. To the spectators I may seem fine, but those closest to me know I'm not. Despite the severe muscle spasms, I manage to finish the race and not drown. As my coach pulls me out of the water, he can see that my arms are stiff as a board and that my hands are clenched into fists. I think my eyes speak even louder than my body, and tears begin to run down my face uncontrollably.

During the Games, participants are assigned a different Team USA coach for each event. There is no coincidence that Coach Tom Franke is coaching me today. Coach Tom Franke has already taught me so much about God and having faith and trusting, and he was an incredible help during the classification fiasco. After Coach Tom Franke pulls me out of the water and gets me into my wheelchair, he wraps a towel around me and rushes me away from the yelling reporters and cameras. He acts as a human shield, so the media can't see what a hot mess I am—spasming and crying. They have already said enough about me and offered one too many opinions and comments. Coach Tom Franke finds a quiet space and kneels down in front of me. I can barely speak between sobs. I didn't make the final; I won't be winning a medal and am devastated. For any athlete, defeat is inevitable and heartbreaking. But when it is on the world stage, when everyone is watching, it is even more devastating. Not making it to the finals when I was supposed to medal is a tough pill to swallow.

"I, I, I, let everyone down. I'm so sorry."

He looks at me and shakes his head. "You have not let anyone down, Victoria, this was not your fault. It's been a long week, and today wasn't your day. But guess what?"

"What?"

"You now have two full days to rest and get ready for your

next race, which is *your race*: the one hundred freestyle." Coach Tom Franke is right. Deep down I know that there is a reason for this. I know I don't have a chance to win gold in the breaststroke, but I do have a chance to win the 100 freestyle. There is definitely something to be said about having two full days to rest and prepare. The last week was so stressful and chaotic that I really haven't had a lot of time to prepare for my races. I have yet to arrive to a race in the right mind-set because of all the chaos and noise of the media and IPC classification issues.

So, in many ways, this loss is a gift from God. It is not a setback but instead a setup for a greater comeback. That is something I learned from Joel Osteen, one of my favorite Christian authors. Finally, I will have some peace and quiet and time to get in my zone. I take this time to also count my blessings and remember why I love to swim. I don't swim for sponsors like some do. I swim for God, my family, and especially for my grandma, who managed to recover from major surgery to be here in London to watch me. She's believed in me from the very beginning and has always encouraged me, even when I was deathly ill. It is for these reasons that I am here and why I am ready to shine.

It's MY time.

I've always been nervous and excited on race days. I go over my race and anxiously await my time to swim. I nervously pack and then repack my swim bag and pace around in my wheelchair. But this day is different. I wake up not thinking about my race at all.

I think about how beautiful it is outside and how excited I am to be in the Olympic Village. I hold on to my Team USA swim cap and remember being a little girl and dreaming of having a Team USA swim cap with "Arlen" on the side. I did it. I am here, and for the first time in nearly two weeks, it all sinks in. I am past the heartbreak and drama and chaos that have shadowed my life and swimming and the Games. For the first time, I feel how I think all the other athletes are feeling.

Excited.

Amazed.

I can finally say *I made it.*

I know this day is different from all the others because I am so relaxed and calm and excited. The lightness and joy that I've been missing ever since I touched down in London have now returned. I am ready, more ready than I have ever felt before.

This is MY time.

I feel a powerful confidence that can be credited only to God. I know deep down that this race is going to be different. In my two days off, I had managed to meet with the team's sports psychologist (which was a game changer), and I also took some much-needed time to be quiet and pray. Even during some of my toughest battles in this journey, I have found peace in God. Trusting, believing, and handing it over to Him have helped me survive and get to this point.

Despite being incredibly superstitious, I have a whole new

approach and focus for my race. Aside from my chocolate chip cookie dough PowerBar, blue Gatorade, lucky goggles, race suit, and replaying the race in my mind, I now have a new addition to my routine. I break the race down into a four-point checklist: *start, break out, turn,* and *finish.* That is all I need to focus on.

"Take your mark . . ."

BEEP!

Within seconds, I am in the water. Checklist time.

Start . . . check.

As soon as I reach the surface, I begin to move my arms as quickly and efficiently as possible, grabbing for as much water possible with each stroke.

Break out . . . check.

Before I know it, I'm at the wall. With the 100 free, the turn is the most crucial part in maintaining, gaining, or even losing the lead. Ellie and the other swimmers are trailing behind, and one swimmer from Germany is almost neck-and-neck with me. This turn needs to be perfect.

Turn . . . check.

This is it, this is *my* moment. All those tears and all that heartbreak fuel me and ignite a fire within that had been lost many years ago.

Come on, Victoria.

Unlike any of my other races in London, where I could hear the crowd and was entirely aware of the swimmers around me, this time it's as if I'm in another place. Part of my routine—and probably one of the key things that helps me stay focused—is singing the song "Good Life" by OneRepublic. OneRepublic is my favorite band, and that song was stuck in my head during my first world-record-breaking race. Needless to say, it has stayed with me since. And it resonates in this current situation and allows me to tune out the craziness of the Games.

As I approach the 25-meter mark, in my head, I hear these words from the song:

"This could really be a good life,

A good, good life."

I am overwhelmed with excitement, and it takes every muscle in my body not to smile as I glide through the water. I think about the first time I hit the water two years ago and how scared I was and how my brother William held on to me and encouraged me not to be afraid.

Don't be afraid.

Keep swimming.

Just keep swimming.

You have nothing to lose but everything to gain.

In this very moment—regardless of the outcome of this race— I know that I did it. I made it through. And not only have I survived, I have thrived. Our family has come through one of the toughest and most incredibly heartbreaking situations, and here we all are.

Thank you, God.

I'm so entrenched in gratitude and my song that I don't even realize that I have gained a significant lead and am about a body length ahead of all the other swimmers.

Head down and breathe, Victoria.

You can do this.

"Let's watch the clock; it is a new world record. Victoria Arlen has just won GOLD!"

In one minute and thirteen seconds, I touch the wall first in a world-record time. For a brief moment, it feels as if everything is standing still—the crowd, the water, and I seem to freeze. Quickly I snap back to reality and realize what I have just accomplished.

I did it.

I really did it.

I won.

I had gotten used to coming in second in last week's events. So, seeing my name on the scoreboard with a "1" and a "WR" (world record) shocks me, and I feel so *emotional.* I look for my family in the crowd; they are high up in the stands, and I know they must be in awe and shock, too. This moment is for them; this whole race is for them. All the tears we've cried and the pain we've endured has paid off in this very moment. No words can come even close to describing how I feel in this moment and in the moments to come.

Reality hits when I get my medal and see the American flag rise and hear the anthem play. For the first time in this journey, I am ahead of the game. I have spent so much time "catching up." Until this moment, I hadn't known what it is like to win and be ahead. This moment changes everything for me.

I even get a compliment from Coach John, who is watching in the States. "Good job, kid, that was a perfect race." And that is icing on the cake. Before connecting with my family, I go back to my space in the locker room. The place where I'd cried one of my most painful cries, and the place where I prayed so passionately. I take a moment, hold my medal, and close my eyes.

Thank you, God.

This one's for you.

You're the true gold medalist.

People think that the gold medal is the best part of the Games. Now, don't get me wrong; it's incredible. But an even better moment is seeing the people you love the most afterward. The glory is fun, the anthem is amazing, the crowds are electric. But when you see your daddy, mummy, brothers, aunties, grandparents, and friends—that's a whole other level of awesome. The people you love the most, who fought so hard for you to achieve your dream, who believed in you . . . this is their glory. We had gone through hell, but now we have made it to our happy place. Tears of joy instead of pain, embraces of congrats and joy instead of embraces of fear that this might be the last time. Now it was time to start living.

You're back, Victoria.

Time to live.

• • •

The next few months—from October to May—are a blur of appearances and media obligations, learning to drive with hand controls, as well as returning to school. I am in my senior year, and all of a sudden, the kids who made fun of me and treated me terribly want to be my friends. Apparently, a gold medal makes a person way cooler.

For the first time since I was eleven, I am treated "normal" at school. Although it's crazy that I had to get a gold medal to be accepted, I am incredibly thankful to have my senior year (despite the newfound fame and craziness) be somewhat normal. Then again, my "normal" is not most people's normal.

Class of 2013:

Cameron Arlen.

Victoria Arlen.

William Arlen.

The gold medal was amazing, but graduating on time and with my triplet brothers feels just as amazing. I missed sixth grade through my freshman year of high school, so simply getting back to school has been overwhelming—with so many odds against me and mountains to climb. But thanks to my family, friends, a handful of teachers, and a kick-butt case manager and guidance counselor, I was actually able to catch up.

Many of the teachers who doubted me (there were a lot of

them) just didn't understand why I was racing to make up five years in three years. But from the moment I realized I was locked in, I felt left behind. My family was there for me and never "left me behind," but life went on for them. So, when I came back, I didn't just want to go with the flow, I wanted to catch up on all that I had lost. I didn't want to sit on the sidelines, I wanted to get back in the game.

But there is still so much I don't understand, and in time will have to slow down to figure out.

11

THIS COULD HAVE
BEEN AVOIDED

June 2013

Why?

One question has plagued my brain since the first day I felt that intense stabbing pain on my right side.

WHY?

No doctor or specialist has ever given me a straight answer to this question. They know that my paralysis is from the transverse myelitis, but none of them can tell me why I went into a vegetative state. My state was labeled as an "encephalitis of unknown origin." Since I woke up, I live every day with the fear of relapsing and the curiosity of "Why?" Although I have made almost a complete recovery aside from being paralyzed from the waist down, I cannot shake the anxiety about the unknown.

Why has this happened to me?

What exactly happened to me?

Will it happen again?

In search of answers, I make an appointment with one of the top TM doctors in the world at Johns Hopkins Hospital, in Baltimore, Maryland. Now, I'm not the biggest fan of doctors, and so making this appointment with a specialist is a big step for me. My mummy and grandma accompany me, but I decide that I need to go into the exam room alone. The specialist is incredibly kind, and I instantly like and trust him. He listens carefully to my account of what's happened to me, and he pulls up my old brain scans. I wait to hear the same script that every other "specialist" has given me.

Never in a million years do I expect what he actually says: "You had ADEM, which stands for acute disseminated encephalomyelitis. You were a textbook case." He goes on to explain that ADEM is part of the TM family and that the combination of the two is what nearly killed me. The damage on my brain and spine scans is clear as day. I am relieved to have an answer and to finally know exactly what happened to me. Each of these conditions is rare, and the combination of the two is even rarer.

Back in 2006 when I got sick, there was little knowledge about TM and ADEM—except for in specialty places like Johns Hopkins. It wasn't until 2010 that more doctors and hospitals began to learn more about the two conditions. However, as with any neurological disorder, being proactive is key. And none of the doctors I'd seen up until now had been proactive.

ADEM is an autoimmune condition, which means that the body's immune system mistakenly identifies its own healthy cells and tissues as foreign and mounts an attack against them. According to the National Multiple Sclerosis Society,

> ADEM is a brief but intense attack of inflammation (swelling) in the brain and spinal cord and occasionally in the optic nerves. This inflammation damages the brain's myelin (the white coating of nerve fibers). Other terms used to refer to ADEM include "post-infectious encephalomyelitis" and "immune-mediated encephalomyelitis."[*]

Transverse myelitis is a similar condition and causes inflammation of the spinal cord.

The perfect storm.

Most, if not all, cases of ADEM and TM are separate. A patient may get one or the other, but usually not both. Both of these conditions struck abruptly and suddenly—within a month of each other—like a twister on a prairie that wreaks havoc, uprooting buildings and destroying everything in its path. ADEM and TM

---

[*] https://www.nationalmssociety.org/What-is-MS/Related-Conditions/Acute-Disseminated-Encephalomyelitis-(ADEM).

severely crippled my life and brought horrific pain and loss. They stole my innocence and many years from my life. And I'm still trying to pick up the pieces from that tornado.

Getting an answer brings a mixture of happiness and relief along with sadness, confusion, and anger. As I try to grasp the doctor's words, nothing prepares me for what comes next.

"This could've been avoided."

He tells me that a simple round of steroids could have prevented this inflammatory process from destroying my body and nearly taking my life. It would've been my best shot at anything close to recovery at the time of the initial onset. My heart sinks, and I don't know if I want to cry, scream, or punch something. My head spins as I begin to process this news. I recognize this feeling of panic and distress and remember feeling this when I was locked in. I feel frozen, absolutely frozen on a merry-go-round that would not stop spinning.

Spinning.

Over and over again.

Breathe, Victoria.

Just breathe.

As I begin to calm down, I learn that if my previous doctors had been proactive, rather than saying my illness was psychological, I maybe would not have gotten sick, and I would not have lost all that I've lost. The initial onset of my illness was quite slow, which would have made me a perfect candidate for treatment and a relatively positive outcome with little to no residual effects. In most cases, ADEM and TM strike quickly, and within a few hours the victim has lost all function, and treatment may not be as effective. However, my medical decline initially was slow, and it was more than likely that I would have responded quite well to treatment. But I did not receive the correct diagnosis; instead, various doctors taunted me, degraded me, and told me I was crazy—for years.

I wasn't crazy.

Those doctors told me I was crazy when they could have and should have helped me. All of those frantic emergency visits and all the condescending remarks were completely unnecessary. The unmarked facility was completely unnecessary. All those years lost—unnecessary.

I'm not crazy.

For years, I was confused about why all of those nurses and doctors called me crazy. Although deep down I knew I wasn't, after hearing it so many times, a part of me secretly wondered and worried.

I'm not crazy.

I'm not crazy.

I'm not crazy.

Over and over again, I mutter these words, hoping each time that I will believe it. As I try to catch my breath, I feel both angry and relieved. I slowly begin to cry, as this truth sinks in.

Believe it, Victoria.

You're not crazy.

You never were.

The rest of the appointment is a bit of a blur. "I'm not crazy"—those three words keep replaying over and over in my mind, drowning out what is said afterward. My mummy joined the appointment after I was given the news, and she later tells me that the doctor gave us some information about potential rehabilitation options for my legs. But he also told us that the likelihood of me walking was slim and that we shouldn't "mortgage the house" for treatment. It was more so to help my scoliosis and the other medical complications that come with being paralyzed from the waist down. I was in horrific pain, and he wanted to see if rehabilitation could possibly help.

The car ride back with my mummy and grandma is quiet. I anxiously look through the packet of information that the doctor gave me, which describes ADEM and TM. I see the diagnoses, and I can't help but feel overwhelmed with emotions. Finally, I have answers. Finally, I can move forward. I can grieve and process the turbulent journey that has consumed the last seven years of my life.

Closure.

It's strange to finally know what happened to me, but it is also horribly upsetting. Now I know that I did not need to go through what I went through—all this could've been avoided. Finding peace has just become even harder, because none of this had to happen.

Breathe, Victoria.

It's okay.

You're okay.

You cannot rewrite the past.

There are many times in life when we don't understand why bad things happen. Whether at the hand of others or damaging acts of nature or something else—there is no quick fix when it comes to processing and healing. Each of us has a different approach, and that is how it should be.

My reaction to painful things is to bottle up my feelings and keep them inside. But when circumstances and feelings come to an irrepressible boil, I finally break down.

But it would be a while before I finally break down.

12

EXHILARATION AND DEFEAT ON THE WORLD STAGE

August 2013 to September 2013

After my successes in London, I take only a week off to see my family, who live in Scotland. As soon as I touch down in Boston, it's "back to work." Back to 3:00 a.m. wake-up calls and back to long, grueling workouts with my coach. According to Coach John, "One gold is not enough."

The racing season picks back up after the New Year, and I set my sights on the 2013 World Championships in Montreal, Canada. I'm excited to see what my times will be now that I have a solid year of training behind me and am no longer a rookie. In London, I had zero experience competing on an international stage, and there is a massive difference between competing nationally (maybe fifty to one hundred people in the stands) versus internationally (twenty-two thousand in the crowds and millions watching on television). Most large sporting events are accompanied by lots of media and drama. I am praying that there will be no drama at the World Champs so that I can just enjoy being a part of Team USA and focus on swimming.

Unfortunately, that will not be the case.

The IPC classifiers are not finished with me yet. In spite of the massive amount of medical documentation I've already submitted and the grueling evaluation they put me through in London, they are not letting up. It was decided that a year from my last classification evaluation (September 2012) I would be reevaluated to make sure everything adds up. The World Champs are in August, so I'm thinking I won't have to worry about classification issues until after the Champs, in September. But . . .

"They decided that they are not going to wait until September and want to classify you in August," I am told very matter-of-factly by our team manager, Queenie.

"You've got to be kidding me."

Please be kidding.

In my opinion, it is beyond wrong to bring up classification during major events. Doing so messes with athletes' heads and throws them off their game. Who knows what I could have done in London if I hadn't experienced such a rough time with the classifiers. It honestly took until the very last night of competition for me to feel like myself and feel excited and relaxed.

So, I am dead set on making sure what happened in London doesn't happen again. I don't want to compete and then be humiliated again. My times are fast, and I am setting world records left and right in practice. My US coaches are very excited and keep encouraging me to go to the World Champs. Several coaches assure me that what happened in London won't happen again and that this new evaluation is just a "formality."

After a while, I believe what I am being told and agree to compete at the Champs. John and I have gotten into a groove, and I am beyond excited to compete—especially now that I have so much training behind me. Sponsors are beginning to take notice, and the "Road to the Rio Paralympics" advertisements and media teasers have already started.

My main competition is not swimming her best, and her times get worse post-London. As much as I don't want to assume or be overconfident, I am confident that I can beat her in Montreal. It will be another showdown of the teenagers, but this time we'll be on even ground. I have caught up in regard to training and maybe even passed her a little bit. I'm not the comeback kid anymore. Instead, I am the one to beat.

• • •

The 2013 World Championships in Montreal are going to be *my* event, and I have worked my butt off to get here. My family and friends have sacrificed their time and energy and have supported me endlessly. I am fueled by their support, so in spite of significant elbow and shoulder injuries from overuse, I keep pushing. Meanwhile, my family has spoken with various US coaches, lawyers, and officials and are aware of the IPC drama.

In retrospect, I can see warning signs of the intentions of the IPC and its CEO to bar me from competition. First, I am not included in the marketing video, which announced the Montreal World Championships, even though I am one of the most talked-about swimmers post-London. Second, Ellie Simmonds *is* included, in spite of the fact that I surpassed her in two out of the three races. I would be her greatest and—given her times—only rival competitor to put her placement at risk. It is also interesting that Ellie did not achieve qualifying times in World Championship trials for the 50 freestyle or the 100 freestyle, yet she was granted a "discretionary" position to compete.

I place no blame on Ellie for any of this. She and I enjoy sharing our competitive spirits, and I respect her tremendously. The fault lies well above either of our heads.

Another warning sign comes in June. Weeks before the competition in Montreal, my family and I receive a concerned email from WMUR, an ABC affiliate. WMUR had reached out through email to the IPC in preparation to send a crew to follow the World Championships and to cover my races. They ask for a schedule of my events. The IPC emails WMUR back saying that

I am not competing in the World Championships. This is before any concerns for my classification have been presented to any of my coaches or to me. When the US Paralympic officials question the IPC, the IPC states that it was an accident that my name was not included and that they must've missed my name. My last name begins with an A. I am at the top of the list.

Even with these issues, never in a million years do I imagine that what goes down would actually go down. I have been assured by the United States Olympic Committee that what happened in London would *not* happen again. In truth, they were right . . . this is *worse* than London.

Since I have been told that my upcoming meeting with the IPC is just a formality appointment, I decide to trust that everything will work out. Of course, I'm anxious, but I channel that anxiety into my training and getting prepared to make my country proud. After all, being a member of Team USA is an honor, and I want to be there for my teammates.

Before I know it, I am on a plane to Montreal. I want to be excited, but my apprehension kicks in.

Is this going to be like London all over again?

Will I be able to swim?

It's true that I am swimming significantly faster than Ellie, but it isn't because I'm cheating. I had chosen not to take a long break after London and had worked really, really hard. The main difference between now and a year ago is that then I had only about five months of solid training under my belt. I had not tapped into my potential in the water. Now I have some serious training behind me, as well as a team supporting me and helping me train and compete at the highest level. I have done my job and have poured everything and every moment of every day into this sport. All those early morning wake-up calls, leaving prom early so I could be rested for double sessions early the next morning, not having a social life—all of it was for this event and the events that would follow—including the 2016 Rio Paralympics.

But in the end, all that hard work and determination gets me nowhere but into a car back home to New Hampshire.

Hope.

Even though the IPC has well over a hundred pages of medical documentation regarding every detail of my disability, they still want more.

My appointment at Johns Hopkins the month before was partly to get information for my peace of mind, but I also thought that surely a diagnosis from this respected institution would satisfy the IPC. And my doctor at Johns Hopkins did provide another concrete diagnosis that I am paralyzed.

Because he was so kind and thorough, I also asked him another question—one that has plagued me for years and continues to be in the back of my mind. I asked what my chances might be of regaining function in my legs and maybe even walking again. Very kindly, he told me that I could try rehab, and he shared some recent spinal cord research findings. But he also said that it would honestly take a "miracle" for me to walk again.

When I asked the doctor that simple question, I had no idea it would create the tidal wave of events that followed. And I never imagined that having "hope" would ultimately ruin and take away the very thing that gives me so much hope.

As it turns out, the IPC uses the doctor's notes to classify me as ineligible. Because I have expressed hope that I want to walk again and regain function, the IPC uses my hope to oust me from the 2013 World Championships. His notes are taken out of context and misinterpreted. The IPC disregards all my other medical records and previous classification examinations. My disabilities are diminished, dismissed, and declared "not permanent." Apparently, the IPC has found a loophole through which they can determine my disability isn't permanent due to the mere fact that I have hope to find a cure for paralysis and gain back mobility.

"What do you mean, I can't swim? I was told you wouldn't let that happen again!"

Not again.

Please.

At this awful meeting, I am pronounced ineligible for classification: "Victoria, you have to go home. You can't be here anymore. Please go pack your bags."

This is cruelly done at 4:30 p.m. Friday afternoon with competition to begin Sunday morning—clearly not allowing enough time to prepare an appropriate appeal. As I leave this meeting with the "matter-of-fact" words and lack of information and explanation, I am numb. I sit in front of my hotel door, shaking and crying, trying to find the strength to scan my key and open the door. I collapse on my bed as my phone rings over and over again, but I have no strength to answer it.

Unable to move, I stare at my race suit and my Team USA swim cap. It is laid out perfectly on my dresser; my lucky goggles' mirrored reflection stares back at me.

How could this happen?

How?

I think about my roommate who is still at practice, and I think about my team and the fun they're having as they train and check out the competition's pool. The IPC wouldn't even let me go to the pool with my team. They made me feel like a prisoner with an incurable disease. Broken, alone, confused, and absolutely devastated, I muster up the energy to pack my things.

I purposely do not go near my swim stuff until everything else is packed. When I do reach for it, I'm overwhelmed with anger, and I throw my race suits, caps, and goggles across the room. As I do, I fall out of my chair and hit my head on the corner of the table. But I don't care.

You can't get much lower than this.

I don't know what to feel. I curl up in a ball and stare blankly at the wall. Closing my eyes, I just want to be woken up from this nightmare.

This can't be happening.

This can't be real.

Wake up, Victoria!

Wake up!

The worst nightmares are the ones you don't wake up from . . .

This is real.

The rule book says it is mandatory that they evaluate me. But they had refused, and their timing ensures that their decision cannot be sent to an appeals court.

So, I go home. There is nothing that can be done and everyone's "hands are tied." That is it. No fighting, no appeals court.

In the blink of an eye, everything is over. Just moments ago, I was a world-record breaker, nominee for an ESPY (Excellence in Sports Performance Yearly) Award, and gold-medal-winning champion swimmer. Now, the sponsors who had been pursuing me stop calling, and my name is plastered all over the media for not being "disabled enough." Which is a cruel and senseless misinterpretation of what actually happened.

As much as this isn't my fault, I feel as if I've let my team down. I am one of the top medal contenders for these games, and people are relying on me. I have fans from all over the world who are looking to me for hope and ready to cheer me on. I have a coach and a family who believe in me and have sacrificed so much.

It's over.

Within two hours of receiving this devastating news, I am in a car—driven by our team manager—to meet my mummy. I am numb, completely numb. I have cried so much that I have no tears left and cannot even formulate words. I sit in the backseat in silence, staring into oblivion and listening to "Oceans (Where Feet May Fail)" by Hillsong United over and over again:

> *"And I will call upon your name*
> *And keep my eyes above the waves . . ."*

God, where are you?
Can you even hear me?
I'm in the deep ocean . . . and I'm drowning.
Please save me.

But sometimes, anger clouds our ability to hear God and understand His purpose.

I keep searching and searching, but my anger, frustration, and confusion are louder than my prayers. I can't stop thinking about the reality of my situation and my swimming career.

What happens now?
Where do I go from here?
Is this it?
Am I done?
Is it really over?

When I get home that night, I am desperate and confused and don't know where to turn or what to do. I find myself hysterically crying on the bathroom floor in the middle of the night. Shaking with anger and confusion.

Detoxing can be hell.

What no one knows is that swimming is my drug. Though I truly love it, it is also the way I cope with the pain of what happened to me. With each stroke, I swim away from the internal battles and the fears that have plagued me since the day I woke up in 2009.

My fix has been suddenly and abruptly taken away from me, and now I am desperate for that drug and that escape. What swimming did for me was beyond the medals and fame and sponsors. It brought me back to life and to the world. For the two to three hours that I train each day, I am actually happy. Through swimming, I can escape the memories, the pain, and the very real post-traumatic stress that I feel. I don't want to be in a wheelchair or in my own head. I want to be in the water, but now I feel like a sword has stabbed me in the chest and is never removed—continually piercing my heart.

I, I, can't do this.

I, I, need to swim.

I have come so far, and now I have been knocked back into my hurt. All for what?

I soon find out losing the very thing that gave me a purpose and a place to escape is the catalyst that changes everything.

Why did they do this to me?

Because I have *hope*, the very thing that kept me alive all those years ago. What I clung to the most ultimately gets me kicked out of the Paralympics. The IPC has been incredibly unreasonable throughout this entire ordeal and, frankly, my entire Paralympic swimming career. Failing to provide concrete reasoning and backed by rules they can't explain for their actions. It makes no sense why I cannot swim. Quickly, I am contacted by some of the top sports lawyers in the country, and they each tell me that I have a "very strong case." And I'm not going to lie, the thought does cross my mind to take legal action, but if I did my hands would literally be tied.

I'd never be allowed to share my story.

In the end, I decide not to pursue legal action in hopes that my swimming career can still be saved without being held up in the legal system. But none of that matters as the IPC refuses to change its position, and still provides what I believe to be illegitimate reasoning. As preposterous as it sounds, I was pushed out because I had hope. And I refuse to let anyone take that away from me.

13

MY ALMOST-QUARTER-LIFE CRISIS

September 2013 to April 2015

"You need to make another statement about the IPC and what happened in Montreal."

I'm done talking.

"Please, just tell everyone to leave me alone."

It's been a month since my world imploded and my swimming career was derailed, and the questions keep coming. Over and over again, I am asked for statements and answers about my declassification in Montreal and the World Championships. But the only answer I can come up with is . . .

I was penalized for having hope.

The life I had worked the last two years to build has now imploded. Between the doctor's words that all my pain and suffering could have been avoided and the realization that my swimming career no longer exists, I find myself slowly slipping away. I don't fully realize it at the time, but I am losing myself.

"But, Victoria . . . *you have it all*. You should be happy."

Perceptions about others are frequently based on assumption. But reality is often very different from what can be seen on the outside. People post "happy" pictures on social media yet are often unhappy and lost on the inside. We create façades to cover up our truth.

"Victoria?"

"Victoria?"

"Yes?"

"Are you okay?"

"Um, yeah. I'm fine . . ."

"Victoria, people are asking a lot of questions. They want answers."

"I have nothing more to say."

Actually . . . I'm not at all fine. I'm slowly drifting away . . .

I'm losing myself again. I thought I had rebuilt everything. I thought my foundation was on solid ground. But I look down at my feet, and all I see is sand, shifting sand—not stone. People often talk about having a midlife crisis. Since I'm only nineteen, how about an almost-quarter-life crisis? This is mine, part one.

Lights out.

Again.

As quickly as the spotlight had turned on, it is turned off.

After the Montreal fiasco, I struggle to find a "new normal." I am surrounded by my family and friends and try to "move on" from swimming.

What the IPC did to me was horrible, but I try to use that as fuel to achieve a new goal: walking. Most of the medical world say my dream of walking is impossible. But I cannot shake the desire to try. After all, I have already achieved several impossible dreams. I can now talk, move, function independently, and ultimately, I have *survived*.

After Montreal, my mummy goes back into proactive mode. My daddy, on the other hand, struggles significantly with what the IPC did to me. He spares no words when speaking to the media and is incredibly frustrated. Like many men, when he can't "fix" something, he gets frustrated and angry. What happened in Montreal is in no way his fault, but he feels responsible to make it all better for me. He struggles to grasp and express his emotions.

When I sense his frustration, I pull away, like I did when I was so sick.

Mummy and I have always been a team, and her relentless efforts to help me take us to San Diego, California, to a facility called Project Walk. Project Walk is a world-renowned spinal cord injury recovery center that specializes in activity-based recovery programs.

Having been to countless rehab and physical therapy clinics, I have a pretty sour taste in my mouth when it comes to "recovery." Most of my previous physical therapy sessions focused on teaching me how to use my wheelchair and live my life in a wheelchair. Don't get me wrong: I needed to learn how to do that. But I didn't want to *stay* in a wheelchair. I wanted to get back on my feet. However, the odds were against me, and my physical therapists didn't believe it was a beneficial route to pursue.

So, when I arrive at Project Walk, I am pretty skeptical and weary.

This is not what I expected.

I am in for a very pleasant surprise. The people at Project Walk are the first people in seven years to give us even a glimmer of hope. They offer no guarantees, but they also don't talk about what's impossible; instead, they focus on what *is* possible.

During our three months in California, we stay with one of my mom's dearest friends, whom I call my West Coast Mamma. (Thank you, Marylynn and Jack.) Just being away from all the drama and resting in their gracious home is healing.

Within the first twenty minutes at Project Walk, I am sweating and being pushed like never before. I am hooked. It is set up like a gym, and I see several individuals, all with different kinds of spinal cord injuries and neurological conditions. We all arrive in wheelchairs, but as soon as our sessions start, we are out. Workouts are adapted to our individual needs. And each of my trainers knows just how far to push me. I love it!

Walking is still a long shot, and during my three months at Project Walk, my eyes are definitely opened to the severity of my paralysis. But in the midst of this realization, I am overwhelmed with motivation and hope—which is key to achieving any kind of "impossible" goal. Trust me: impossible is kind of my thing.

This is the place.

This is where I have my best shot.

Project Walk reignites something in me that has been lost for a very long time. I have not been able to get over or move past my desire to walk again. I'm not ready to accept the idea that I will *never* walk again. More than anything else, I want to look people in the eye and have the freedom to go wherever I want, whenever I want. Thus far, my wheelchair and paralysis have prevented me from doing that. In many ways it feels as if I am trapped in my wheelchair.

Unfortunately, our time at Project Walk must come to an end. Our family and our lives are on the East Coast. It is not practical to live on the West Coast when everyone is back east. So right before Thanksgiving, we head home.

• • •

This is when my life takes a drastic turn for the worse.

Being back home is way more challenging than I anticipate. I struggle with reality and adjusting to a routine. I often drive up north to visit my boyfriend, who is in college, and I try to fit in there.

His friends still see me as the "gold medalist" and still consider me a champion. I want to be treated "normal," yet everywhere I go I seem to be attracting people who crave the spotlight. But I am trying to escape. The attention is cool to them but overwhelming for me. I'm not usually a partier, yet I suddenly find myself surrounded by bad influences.

I think I'm happy, but I'm chasing an illusion. I am trying to numb the pain and sadness that I have yet to acknowledge consciously. And without knowing it, I am walking away from my family and my life and trying to create a different life—one that doesn't hurt so much.

I still have a strong need to swim, so I often find a pool and swim until I'm exhausted. Maybe I'm swimming because I crave the competition and the accolades. Maybe it's to prove to the world that I'm not "washed up." This phrase is used more and more by my friends and boyfriend at the time. And even though they are "joking," words like that sting, especially in my current emotional state.

The best way I know to describe my state of mind is an out-of-control carousel, spinning faster and faster yet going nowhere. Around and around, spinning so fast that I am intoxicatingly dizzy. To the outside world, I am this lucky nineteen-year-old who is being flown all over the country for speaking engagements and appearances. I'm the epitome of "success," but what they do not know is that I'm using it to cover my inner pain and discontent-ment. I am supposed to be this "inspiration, hero, and example," yet that is the last thing I feel. I've become an expert at plastering on a smile and making other people happy. I didn't realize it, but I was beginning a journey down a long road of severe anxiety and depression.

My new friends want to come to events with me, and they praise me for my accomplishments. I find myself wanting to impress them. Over and over again, proving that I was not "washed up."

Put on a smile, Victoria.

Don't cry, at least not in front of anyone.

Don't let them see you "not perfect."

As a baby and as a growing kid, I was happy and joyful and full of laughter. And my family was always happy and laughing. Even when I was deathly ill, my family never lost their humor. To others, I appear joyful and light, but it's just on the surface. It's not real. Deep down, my joy, humor, and light have disappeared. My default and ingrained personality still "works" for me, even when I'm sad. Smiling is a survival tactic. No matter what I am going through or where I am, I know how to turn it on.

My closest friends—and even my family—have no idea that I'm struggling so much. I try not to let anyone see the internal turmoil and discontentment that are building in me. I struggle each day to fight and overcome it, but doing so means I turn up the numbing mechanism I'm becoming so used to. I make sure I stay busy. I fixate on impressing my circle of spotlight seekers, and I work even harder to prove myself.

Keep proving.

I have already achieved so much and come so far, yet that is not good enough. I keep spinning and spinning until . . . God throws me off the carousel, metaphorically speaking.

No, no, no.

This can't be happening . . .

It has been three years since my last seizure. I am off my seizure meds, and the doctors don't think they'll ever come back. The first seizure is small, but it freaks me out. I try my very best to brush it off, but on the inside, I start to worry.

What's happening to me?

On the outside I seem fine, so I don't let myself believe that anything is wrong.

I'm probably just tired.

I push myself, harder, harder, and harder. I'm desperately fighting the internal mayhem and keeping myself so busy that I don't have time to think. I am fixated on going, going, going, and being perfect and successful. And I can't see—don't want to see—what is going wrong with my life. Many of the new people who came into my life so quickly are dysfunctional and don't have my best interests at heart. In fact, they are unknowingly contributing to the emotional mess I've become. I am filled with anxiety and the urge to please and prove.

I am slowly slipping away in more ways than I know—all with a smile on my face.

The seizures become more frequent, and before I know it, I feel sick and tired and anxious all the time.

Slowly losing myself.

Falling further and further into the unknown.

Crashing.

I am overwhelmed and frightened and confused. My world is imploding, and there is nothing I can do to stop it. Yet I continue to try to balance it all and make everyone happy.

But now that I'm becoming more physically limited, my new friends begin to disappear like moths that fly off into the night when you shut off the light. My boyfriend and "friends" have lost interest in me, dumping me and kicking me to the curb.

I truly feel washed up.

I need to get off the carousel that won't stop spinning. Not only am I emotionally shutting down, but my body is shutting down, too.

This is what sinking to the bottom feels like.

Have you ever done a pencil dive? Jumping into the water (deep water) as straight as a pencil? You jump and then you sink—fast. You either reach the bottom or go deeper than a normal jump can take you. And when you get to the bottom, you frantically swim up, the bounce in your body quickly propelling you upward, and you break through the surface and breathe.

But have you ever stayed under a little too long? Your ears pop and your lungs contract and your mind races. You are filled with panic, and you fight your way to the surface.

I don't know how to make the panic and the racing mind stop.

I had jumped into the fast life and gone straight to the bottom. But I'm not being propelled back to the surface. I can't breathe; I'm drowning . . . I'm pulled wherever the water pulls me, and I'm thrashed around by every wave. There is no set path or strength in this wayward sailboat. I crash over and over again, and I never reach shore. Going and going, but never ending up anywhere. Eventually, this internal battle begins to surface.

H . . . E . . . L . . . P . . .

The seizures become even more frequent. I'm losing my "sparkle." My body aches, and it gets harder and harder to get out of bed and find any semblance of joy. Up until now, I'd been able to fake it, but I can't keep up the façade. One of my biggest fears is coming to life—relapsing.

I need a break, an escape from the crazy world I've created. Appearances, events, competitions, fake people, drama, and pressure have literally owned my life for the past two years (2012 to 2014). All of a sudden, the "spotlight" goes off, and like a car without headlights, I crash hard and fast into the rocky bottom, the dark unknown.

I heard a quote a long time ago that goes something like this: "Many people want to ride with you in the limo, but only true friends take the bus with you when the limo breaks down." The

It was a buy two get one free kind of day in the Arlen household.
(Courtesy of the Arlen family)

Three is better than one.
(Courtesy of the Arlen family)

Not much has changed.
(Courtesy of the Arlen family)

The three musketeers.
(Courtesy of the Arlen family)

Since day one, LJ has always had my back.
(Courtesy of the Arlen family)

Love my mummy! (Check out that mushroom cut—#90sbaby).
(Courtesy of the Arlen family)

Lake Winnipesaukee with my favorite
humans and my fluffy dog, Jasmine.
(Courtesy of the Arlen family)

The golden years.
(Courtesy of the Arlen family)

Bubble squad.
*(Courtesy of the
Arlen family)*

The Arlen
family circa
1998.
*(Courtesy of the
Arlen family)*

One of the last
photos of the four of
us before I got sick.
*(Courtesy of the
Arlen family)*

Daddy always holds me up.
(Courtesy of the Arlen family)

The annual first day of school photo (third grade).
(Courtesy of the Arlen family)

At fifteen, everyone goes through an awkward stage . . .
mine was just a little more obvious (wink wink).
(Courtesy of the Arlen family)

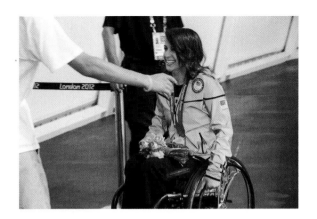

The moment I saw my family after my first medal in London.
(Courtesy of the Arlen family)

The best part about winning a gold medal is not the medal itself, but sharing it with the people you love.
(Courtesy of the Arlen family)

My favorite humans.
(Courtesy of the Arlen family)

Da na na na na na.
(Courtesy of the Arlen family)

Rock Your Disability!™
(Joe Faraoni/ESPN Images)

First day on the job with the legend himself, Michael Phelps.
(Kohjiro Kinno/ESPN Images)

My first red carpet at the 2013 ESPYS.
(Scott Clarke/ ESPN Images)

ABOVE: I would not be standing without my trainer, John (left) and my mummy (right). (April 2016)
(Courtesy of the Arlen family)

LEFT: Ten years after being paralyzed and thanks to my trainers John and Daniele, I was able to show my wheelchair who's boss.
(Courtesy of the Arlen family)

Standing in front of thousands at America's Night of Hope in Detroit with Joel Osteen was a moment I will for sure never forget. This was a moment where I truly learned the power of sharing my story and spreading hope.
(Lakewood Church)

The bottom of the super-pipe at the X Games
(I still have to pinch myself sometimes).
(Eric Lars Bakke/ESPN Images)

Top of the mountain—there's no greater feeling.
(Courtesy of the Arlen family)

The moment it all hit me, right after my first dance on *Dancing with the Stars*. *(Courtesy of the Arlen family)*

My *Dancing with the Stars* partner in crime: Valentin Chmerkovskiy. *(© 2017 American Broadcasting Companies, Inc. All Rights Reserved.)*

When two worlds collide: by far one of the most memorable moments when paying tribute to the sport that I hold closest in my heart and turning the ballroom into a hockey rink.
(© 2017 American Broadcasting Companies, Inc. All rights reserved.)

This photo was taken moments before our Most Memorable Year dance.
It was a moment that the viewers at home didn't see. It perfectly captured
who Val is as a dance partner and friend. This was the first time in
this entire journey where I truly found a purpose for the pain.

I honestly don't really have words for this one.
This was a surreal moment, but also a moment
of triumph and healing for me. A moment when
my journey came full circle on the ballroom
floor—wheelchair and all.

Wouldn't be anywhere
without these two.

What a way to celebrate your twenty-third birthday. Forever thankful to my *Dancing with the Stars* family, and to Taylor Swift for the amazing bouquet of flowers.
(Courtesy of the Arlen family)

After watching *The Ellen Show* religiously every day from my hospital bed, it was really crazy to come full circle and be on her show.
(Courtesy of the Arlen family)

From the swimming pool to the dance floor, Coach John has been one of my biggest supporters.
(Courtesy of the Arlen family)

Robin has been an incredible inspiration of mine (also our shoe game is on point).
(Courtesy of the Arlen family)

ABOVE: Snuggled up on set at X Games Aspen 2018.
(Joe Faraoni/ESPN Images)

LEFT: We have been on quite a journey. Beyond grateful to have had these two through every step of the way.
(Courtesy of the Arlen family)

limo has indeed broken down, and I feel abandoned on the street. The ones who stand by you through the worst of times are the best ones to celebrate with in the best of times.

The "world" I'd built has come tumbling down, and I am buried in the rubble. I've lost a significant amount of weight, and I literally cannot get up. Once again, I find myself on the floor. I push my wheelchair away and cry uncontrollably.

How did I get here?

How could I let this happen?

When I was really sick, I was physically and mentally "locked in." I couldn't move or talk or function. It was a prison sentence for a crime I hadn't committed. When I came back, I came back with a vengeance, never truly understanding what had happened to me or the effects of the trauma I had endured. Never dealing with the sadness, the loss, and the abuse. Yet, I came back with a smile and the desire to just move on.

Just forget.

All of it.

Remembering those painful places hurt too much; the pain was like a piece of glass in my foot, stabbing me with each movement. When the pain begged to be tended to, I would be too "busy." I was desperate to forget. But if you walk around with a piece of glass in your foot, you'll eventually be forced to remove it. It will hurt so much that you can't take it anymore, and you'll have to sit down and deal with it.

Sit down, Victoria.

Slow down, Victoria.

Are you okay, Victoria?

No.

In the first few months of 2014, I am running as fast as I can, smiling and grinning on the outside, but steadily deteriorating on the inside. Now I can't breathe, and I am a slave to the seizures.

Knocked. Back. Down.

In many ways it feels as if this new life has failed me. I have nothing to look forward to and can't bear to look back. I am stuck between two worlds: the now and the past. Pain versus pain.

I vividly remember my mummy walking into my room, and— like she always does—she lifts me up. "Mummy's here, you *will* get through this. I promise." My mom has always been my rock, through the good and the bad. She has always been there for me, even when things were the scariest. Her strength and perseverance have never wavered. If anything, when things got tough, she shined the brightest. I've always admired her for that. Her strength, joy, and love are the most powerful things I've ever known.

My mummy sees how broken I am. She has watched me slowly slip away from my family, but she is trying to "give me space," which I had pleaded for. But she never stops watching out for me. She fears that a day would come when I'd "crash." I would call what I am experiencing more an implosion than a crash. But she is there to pick up the pieces. I'm not the only one who experiences my trauma—she experiences it, too.

Mummy and I have been on this insane journey with incredible highs and devastating lows. Once the swimming ended, we both struggle with our purpose and place. It had been "our thing" to travel together to practices and meets, but after swimming abruptly ended, I ran away from both the pool and her. We'd always been so close, but after Montreal and swimming ended I drifted away from everyone. I was trying to hide my pain and sadness from the ones I love the most.

That is NEVER good.

We eventually figure out that my seizures are a reaction to a medication that one of my doctors had prescribed in hopes of preventing a relapse. It takes some time, but after removing the medication and returning to holistic medication, I can feel myself rising back up. Slowly, I push the debris aside and try, once again, to find a new normal. It isn't easy, but over time things begin to improve.

Just try.

Clean slate.

But what's next?

When you don't know where to go, there are two different paths you can take. You can sit down and feel hopeless and not even try, or you can stand up (even though you might feel wobbly) and put one foot in front of the other and trust that God will guide you.

———

I had run away from God after Montreal, and it wasn't until I was at the bottom that I looked up and found Him again. Trusting, believing, and knowing that He's got me and that He has a plan. Or as Joel Osteen says in my all-time favorite book, *Break Out!* (which totally changed my life), "God has already written every day of your life in His book. He knew exactly when that setback would occur, and the good news is He has already arranged a comeback."

It's time for my comeback.

It's time to take back my life and change my direction.

14

DA NA, NA, NA, NA, NA, NA (ESPN)

March 2014 to December 2015

I've always loved challenges and new adventures—ever since I was a little girl. As a child, I was easily bored, and my friends would tease me about how quickly I'd want to move on and play another game. Moving forward has been important to me for as long as I can remember. Actually, I became addicted to moving forward and being challenged. Maybe it was drive or maybe it was crazy, but going backward became the worst thing I could imagine. It terrified me. I had to go, go, and go—always.

But now where do I go?

I thought I had my life all planned out, but my plans never looked beyond swimming professionally. So, when swimming was forcibly taken away from me, I felt lost, and I began searching and wondering what was next. I had been running (metaphorically speaking) for a while now, but I hadn't thought through where I was running to. Or what I was running from.

Now, at nineteen, I am forced to think about where I want to go. But I truly have no idea.

Swimming on the international stage had been an eye-opening experience. It was amazing and overwhelming to be a champion, but being in that position came with a lot of responsibility. One of the biggest responsibilities was dealing with the media. After trials for the Paralympics and up until a few months after the Montreal fiasco, I was on a whirlwind media tour. For the most part, my experiences were positive, but there were a few (especially after Montreal) that were less than stellar. And it was those few not-so-good experiences that tainted my view of the media world.

Several networks approach me about becoming an "on-air personality," like many former pro athletes. I would still be in the sports world, but instead of swimming, I would be talking about swimming among other sports. I am worn out after all that happened in Montreal, so the thought of being thrown back into the spotlight terrifies me.

The year 2014 was one of the toughest of my life—both physically and emotionally. I was struggling to stay afloat on all levels. And putting on a fake smile and fighting to maintain a persona of "perfection." But as you know, I was far from perfect. Even during the craziness, I am searching and yearning for the next step.

Please, God.

Show me the way.

What do I do now?

For the four years I was in a vegetative state, I was sitting on the sidelines. And I never want to be on the sidelines again. So, I look to God and pray and beg for my next challenge.

Da, Na, Na, Na, Na, Na.

Even though my swimming career has ended abruptly, my speaking career has picked up. Every other week, I am flying to another place and speaking to another crowd. I put on a smile and talk about being victorious over challenges, even though I am far from overcoming anything. People tell me I inspire them, but on the inside, I am lost. I am busy, but I'm not going anywhere.

But then, everything changes once again, with a single speaking event.

One day, my agent Patrick casually asks: "Hey, Victoria, can you go to ESPN and give a few speeches and make a few media appearances?" Being in the speaking and traveling mode, I promptly reply with a yes. I have been doing so much speaking and so many media appearances that this doesn't seem out of the ordinary. I grew up watching ESPN, but being in the funky head space I am in, even this doesn't excite me. The only thing that stands out is that the guy I am dating at the time is "obsessed" with ESPN. So this opportunity will impress him.

"Have you ever thought of a career in broadcasting?" asks Mike Heimbach, who is the president of ESPN Global Security.

No.

I've been asked about this many times, and "no" is always my standard answer. But something tells me that this may be different. I sense that Mike sees something that I don't see. He arranges a tour of ESPN to show me around.

"Welcome to SportsCenter."

Being able to watch a live taping of SportsCenter was a "lightbulb" moment for me. I KNEW I wanted to be in that studio. Those four letters had a whole different meaning.

One of the programs I am scheduled to speak on while there is a radio podcast with an anchor by the name of Prim. Prim, like me, is a former elite athlete, and she, too, knows what it's like to transition from sports to broadcasting.

Lightbulb.

The lights, the cameras, the action! All of a sudden, I want to know more. So, I start picking her brain after we record the podcast. Prim is incredibly patient with all of my questions and eagerness, and she even invites me to come back and job shadow her.

Really?

"Of course!" Prim said kindly.

Victoria, you've found your new goal.

Of course, achieving that goal is easier said than done. ESPN is the prize, the finish line, the gold medal for any aspiring sports broadcaster. *Everyone* wants a shot at ESPN. It doesn't get much higher than being a part of that place and having that position on your résumé. Rightfully so, because the place is *insane* and *amazing*, and the energy is electric. Regardless of the odds of landing any kind of job there, I am hooked and want to learn more. I know I want to be there, and that I would do whatever it takes to get there.

A few months later, I begin job shadowing. Each time I come to campus to job shadow, Mike introduces me to various executives and producers. Every person I meet with is incredibly kind, and I make it a point to keep in touch with everyone. Over the next year, I continue to job shadow Prim and other anchors. The fire and passion that were so brutally ripped away from me in Montreal are beginning to flame. I know with every ounce of my body that this is the place I need to be. But . . .

"You're too young."

"You have zero experience."

"We hire people with twenty years of experience, not people who just turned twenty."

"It is unheard of for someone with little to no experience to land an on-air job at ESPN."

The typical path to broadcasting is filled with lots of experience at smaller stations and networks. ESPN is the job at the end of a long, arduous broadcasting journey. You earn your spot through experience. I know all of this, but I also know that when I am pulled so strongly by a specific goal, nothing slows me down.

It is very similar to my experience with swimming. I knew that, because of my lack of experience, the odds of making the US team were slim. And the odds of medaling were even slimmer. But my entire journey has been filled with many "miracles" and "unheard of" instances of success. Perhaps it was, as Joel Osteen taught me, "God paying me back double for the trouble." I believe that overcoming extraordinary odds leads to an extraordinary life. And with great pain comes great gain.

Your time is coming.

I'm not aiming for a job with a fancy title; I just need to be at ESPN. I am willing to get coffee or clean bathrooms just to be there. I even try to convince an executive that I could strap a wagon to my wheelchair and deliver coffees. This might sound crazy, but sometimes pursuing passions makes people a little crazy. But I know that this is where I am meant to be. I just don't know how I would get my foot/chair in the door.

• • •

I have just celebrated the nine-year anniversary of my journey (from April 2006 to April 2015) and my mom says, "Victoria, something amazing is about to happen."

It is April 30, 2015, and my mummy's words echo in my head. I'm not really sure what my mom means, and I certainly don't expect that my life and my path will change that very day. I had met with several executives and producers and individuals who are in big positions at ESPN. But I never go into any of my meetings expecting a job. I simply want advice, and I continue to move forward and learn.

But on April 30, a meeting with Bill Bonnell and Kate Jackson changes everything.

"We want to give you a shot."

"Are you serious? Is this legit?"

Bewildered, excited, and shocked, I sit across from Bill and his producing partner, Kate (both brilliant humans), unsure what to make of what they just said.

"Kate and I would love to have you as part of our broadcasting team for the Special Olympics World Games in LA this summer."

I can't even begin to describe how I feel.

This is my shot.

My next adventure.

Two people who barely know me actually believe in my dream and are willing to take a chance on me. They don't know if I will be good or bad, yet they want to give me a shot. This is the first time in a long time that I've met with someone who believes in me. I don't think Bill and Kate realize the significance of that moment for me. I leave the meeting forever changed. I will never forget that moment, and I am eternally grateful for it.

This is your time, Victoria.

The Special Olympics approach quickly. I have spent numerous hours training and working with various coaches to learn how to be an "on-air personality/reporter." This reporting job in Los Angeles will ultimately be my "audition" for ESPN—showing whether or not I have what it takes to make it.

No pressure . . .

Well, actually a lot of pressure.

But . . .

I thrive on pressure.

Sometimes all it takes is one person to believe in you. One cheerleader can be louder than a million naysayers. While in Los Angeles, I have a whole team of cheerleaders. The entire broadcasting team embraces me with open arms. With all their kindness and faith in me, I can't help but thrive and strive to make them proud. They believe in me, so I have to believe in me, too.

Television is daunting, but since I was little, I've loved the camera. As a professional athlete, I never minded on-camera interviews, which many athletes dread. But I hadn't appreciated the position of the interviewer until I was the one with the microphone. It's one thing to be asked the questions, but it's a whole other ball game to be the one asking. I had no idea that so much goes into an interview. And now I am learning not only how to be a reporter but how to be a reporter for ESPN.

I was an Olympics junkie growing up. I idolized the athletes and wanted to be like them one day. But I never imagined that I could be one of them until I actually won the gold in 2012. It has been three years since then, and my love for the Games and the athletes has never wavered. The first Olympics that I remember truly impacting me was the 2004 Summer Games in Athens, Greece. Michael Phelps *crushed* it, and I knew after watching him that I wanted to win gold. Michael Phelps and Jenny Thompson were the swimmers I looked up to. I had gotten the chance to meet and get to know Jenny at an Olympic sponsorship event (first time I was ever starstruck), but I had never met Michael. That is, until my first day on the job at ESPN.

"Victoria, your first official interviewee is going to be Michael Phelps."

Wh—, Wh—, What?!

Just when I think I am already on cloud nine after being handed the ESPN microphone, I am now on an even higher cloud. Cloud nine has turned into cloud nine million.

Michael is my first official interviewee on my first official day at ESPN. It is a features shoot, focusing on the Olympics, Paralympics, and Special Olympics. I am the Paralympian moderator, there is a Special Olympics athlete who represents the Special Olympics, and Michael represents the Olympics. To say I am nervous is an understatement. Michael is by far the greatest Olympian of all time, and I am interviewing him. Me, Victoria Arlen, who as a little girl wanted to be a gold medalist "just like Michael Phelps." And not only am I a gold medalist, but today I have the chance to interview the one who inspired me to become that.

"You're doing great, just be yourself and you'll be just fine."

The first shoot is private and free from the crowds, but at the second shoot, we are surrounded by cameras and crowds, all wanting a piece of Michael. As kids, we always look up to certain people, but there is nothing more wonderful than the person you look up to being exactly who you thought they were, or in this case even better. Michael's kindness, patience, and friendliness show me that he is truly spectacular, and I am forever grateful.

Another notable person on my first day at work is Robin Roberts. For years throughout my vegetative state, I would watch her on *Good Morning America*. Robin was a source of inspiration to me and a familiar start to each morning, when I did not know what the day would entail. My first official debut on ESPN is during the Special Olympics World Games opening ceremonies. Robin arrives on the set early to help with hosting duties. I am a tad starstruck, given that just a few years back, I watched her every morning from my hospital bed. She smiles warmly and introduces herself, then she sits down in front of me. I have prerecorded an intro, and when it airs during the live broadcast, Robin looks back at me and gives me the two-thumbs-up. This is a moment I will definitely never forget.

The rest of the Special Olympics World Games are filled with incredible feats by some of the strongest and most inspirational athletes in the world. I have always been a huge supporter of the Special Olympics movement, and I coached Special Olympians throughout high school. But to see the Games firsthand and to be on the sidelines getting to know the athletes is beyond anything I could imagine.

Life-changing is an understatement.

There is power in sharing someone else's story.

I had never truly known or understood the impact and power of a story until I was the one telling them. Sure, I've spent the last few years sharing my story, but my own story hadn't really impacted me. I was always impacting others and "inspiring" everyone else, yet I was never inspired myself.

This is the first time that I am the one holding the microphone and helping someone else share their story. For a few days, I can put my struggles aside and focus on something else. And after such a turbulent past year, it is refreshing to do so. Here in Los Angeles, I am inspired daily by the athletes' stories. I'll never forget what my dear friend and Special Olympics superstar and ESPN commentator Dustin Plunkett says to me: "If you take the time to speak with the athletes, I can promise you that you will be forever changed and inspired." Dustin is 100 percent right.

That trip is what starts my career at ESPN, but it also reignites a fire inside of me—a fire that for the last year has been all but extinguished. I once again find purpose and inspiration and empowerment.

Forever changed.

After I come home from LA, I am most definitely changed. And now I am back at an ESPN meeting with various executives to discuss how I did in LA and whether or not I have "what it takes" to work there. I still have so much to learn, but I can't think of a better place to learn than the place that ignited the spark for broadcasting.

Do I have what it takes?

Will I get a contract?

Whenever I am passionate about something, I always experience an internal battle of doubt. Especially when my goal is extraordinary and not the normal/easy path. I am often my own loudest naysayer, and my own internal battles can trip me up more than anything else.

But how do I shut off that doubt?

I haven't found a "magic" button that instantly shuts off my doubt, but I have found that if I maintain a habit of believing in myself, over time that viewpoint becomes second nature. If this journey has taught me anything, it's that when I doubt, I am usually on the verge of something amazing. But I have to have faith in God and faith in myself deep, deep down.

Faith and fear do not mix well, and so I'm learning to turn up my faith channel and turn down my fear channel. It's kind of like the way I feel about scary movies versus feel-good movies. Scary movies leave me tense, anxious, and wondering if the monster is going to be under my bed or in my closet at night. (Not a big scary-movie fan.) But feel-good movies leave me feeling inspired and empowered and ready to take on the world.

And it's the same way with faith and fear. Fear fills me with doubt and, well, more fear. But faith gives me hope and courage. And sometimes I have to feel the fear and do it anyway, while holding on to the faith that gives me the courage to fly.

So, when I get back from LA, I am at a crossroads. I now know what I want to do next with my life, but I don't know if I'll get the chance to do it. I have recently turned down the opportunity to go away to college, opting to continue to finish my degree online, and I'm not sure if I made the right choice.

It may sound silly, but part of me just wants to be a normal twenty-year-old, and I'd thought that going away to school would give me that. But something amazing and out of the ordinary always seems to get in the way. In high school it was winning a gold medal and breaking world records, after high school, it was the speaking tours and appearances, then it was Project Walk, and now it's ESPN. Most kids my age go to school to set out a plan for their lives, but the crazy thing is, I already know the life path I want to set out on. It is beyond speaking and beyond swimming. I'm just not sure I know how to get things started.

Waiting.

Wishing.

Wanting.

Patience is not my thing.

It is a beautiful September morning, and I am sitting in the

ESPN welcome center, looking over the full day of meetings planned out for me.

This is it.

This is when it will be decided.

Do I stay at ESPN?

Or go home and go back to the drawing board?

I have been so lost for so long, and for the first time in a long time, I feel like I am found. For the first time since swimming was taken away from me, I am happy and excited about my future. I am no longer looking back at the pool, waiting and wishing things were different. I'm no longer waiting to see if the IPC will change its mind and give me a fair chance. Swimming and the IPC were in my rear window when I was in LA and holding that ESPN microphone. And today I'll find out if I'll be able to continue that passion and move forward.

This is it.

"You know I'd be straightforward with you if I thought you did an okay job in LA. I'd tell you to get an agent and go elsewhere and improve before you can get hired here."

"Yes, I understand."

"But that's not the case here; you belong here. We want to offer you a job here at ESPN."

"Are—are—are you serious?"

"Yes, I'd like to officially welcome you to ESPN."

I had just come out of a pretty tough time. In my search to find new meaning, I forgot the values I'd held all my life. But getting a job offer at ESPN shortly after my twenty-first birthday and becoming one of the youngest on-air personalities ever hired? This whole experience reminded me of how God uses our setbacks as setups for greater comebacks. ESPN gave me a hand and helped me stand up, figuratively. Little did I know that it would also help me physically.

It is time to rise.

15

BACK ON MY FEET—LITERALLY

November 2015 to March 2016

Scars. I define a scar as a reminder—sometimes visible, sometimes not—of a struggle or moment when I was in pain. My journey left several wounds and created many scars, but most of my visible scars from various surgeries and procedures have healed. The scars on my stomach where my GJ tube once resided are hidden behind my clothes; the scars on my back from the inflammation caused by the TM are hidden as well. So, all of my scars are invisible—except for one.

My wheelchair.

When I got better and started to come back to life in 2010, I was told over and over, "You'll never walk again. The damage to your spine is irreversible." It's true that the odds of walking after you've been paralyzed for more than two years are close to none.

But two years into my journey, I was still in a vegetative state. So, I had actually been paralyzed for four years, reducing my chances of regaining function even further.

I thought I had accepted the fact that I couldn't walk. I was grateful to be alive and somewhat "normal." My wheelchair complicated things, but it never really stopped me. I had learned to be independent and had started to find my way when I turned seventeen. But I was not okay with being in a chair when I left the house. Strangers treated me weirdly, and kids at school were cruel. But when I was in the comfort of my home surrounded by my family and friends, I was fine.

However, over time I became less content with my situation. It was hard not walking when all I'd ever known was walking. I knew what freedom felt like, and I found myself longing for it more and more. Some mornings when I was still in the sleepy phase of waking up, I would slide my legs over the bed and start to stand. But, of course, I would crash to the ground, quickly waking up to my reality.

I began to realize that I was lying to myself that I was "okay" with being wheelchair bound. In all honesty, I hated it. It was the ultimate reminder of what had happened to me.

I could never get over the fact that I had literally defied every odd except one: walking. I had survived, I had come back at an incredibly fast rate, and I had begun to live again. I had a life and résumé of experiences and accomplishments beyond most people's wildest dreams.

But I had never gotten back on my feet. My inability to conquer this hurdle haunted me every day that I got out of bed and had to sit in my wheelchair. My chair was my ultimate battle scar.

I tried to make the best of it with pimped-out wheelchairs, great parking, and hilarious moments with my family and friends. Some people feel extremely awkward around a person in a wheelchair. But my family, friends, and I have a sick sense of humor, so we got into some silly shenanigans.

William and Cameron had learned how to operate the wheelchair van and what to do if my feeding pump went off or malfunctioned. It wasn't easy, but they stepped up and were there to help me. Being out in public was difficult at first, and the relentless stares and comments did not help my anxiety.

One day, William, Cameron, and I went out shopping. This was one of our first ventures out together. There was a woman who kept staring at me as I looked at the shirts on a store rack. I just wanted a little normalcy, but this woman was disrupting my plans.

I could tell she wanted to speak with me, but I refused eye contact. When I did look up, she was right there with this slightly crazy-looking smile. "Why are you in a wheelchair?" she asked me with a very childlike high-pitched voice. William and Cameron heard her, and I gave them the "play along eyes."

"What are you talking about?"

She looked confused and tilted her head. "The . . . the wheelchair you're sitting in. What's wrong with you?" That last part got me going.

"Wait, I'm in a wheelchair? No! This can't be happening! William, Cameron, why didn't you guys tell me?!"

William and Cameron rushed in and were quick to play along. "Why did you tell her!" William yelled at the woman, trying not to smile. Cameron grabbed my wheelchair and began to wheel me out of the store. "Great, this is just great. Thanks a lot."

When the coast was clear, all three of us burst into tears of laughter. Moments like that made the wheelchair situation not so bad. It wasn't ideal, but we made it fun and found humor because after all, if you don't laugh, you'll cry.

Now, in retrospect, I realize that the woman most likely had never actually spoken to someone in a wheelchair or did not know how to approach the situation. Most people are pretty curious too. But for me it was so helpful to laugh.

• • •

But despite the "funny" moments and the cool wheelchairs, I am still unsettled. No matter what I do or achieve, I still go to bed and wake up to that one *major* odd that I cannot defy.

But who says you can't do the impossible?

Impossible seems to be "my thing," and who's to say that I can't define what's *possible*? I remember the promise my parents made when I was first grappling with being wheelchair bound. They promised that they would spend their whole lives helping me get back everything that was taken away from me. At the time, they had no idea how that might come about, but they vowed to never stop searching for a cure or some way to get me back on my feet. None of us knew then that three years later we'd get our answer.

I can't shake the nagging feeling that I need to explore my options for walking one day. That feeling just won't leave me and often keeps me up at night.

I know it's true that God often speaks the loudest in the darkest moments. But sometimes I'm so consumed by the dark that I can't see the small light and the determined path He has put in front of me.

"What is it that you truly want, Victoria?"

I want to walk.

"Well then, let's go for it."

My mummy has always had this "anything's possible" attitude. When I was little, my teacher asked what I wanted to be when I grew up, I proudly said, "Gold medalist." The kids laughed; even the teacher tried to hide a snicker. But I kept those words on my poster anyway.

And when I brought that sparkly poster home and showed my mom, she proudly said, "You can be anything, my sweet girl. Go for it." Mummy has *always* been my biggest cheerleader, and so I am not surprised that when I get the opportunity to learn how to walk—or at least attempt to walk—she jumped right on it.

The promise.

My mom and I had gone to the world-renowned paralysis recovery center, Project Walk, in San Diego, California, back in September through November 2013. But our time there was limited because our life and family are on the East Coast. As our last day approaches, the CEO of Project Walk meets with my mummy and me to help us think about next steps with my paralysis recovery. You have to be persistent. Otherwise, you can very quickly lose the progress.

The CEO explains to us that Project Walk is a franchise. And, he tells us, there are no franchises on the East Coast.

Mummy, you just found your calling.

Since my mom was a little girl, she has wanted to help people. And I know for a fact that I got that same passion from her. But she never quite found the right fit. When my brothers and I were younger, she stayed home to take care of us—years of that period were spent taking care of me. But as my brothers and I got older, she still had that nagging feeling of wanting to help others and make a difference. When we were in California, she and I talked often about how we could help others, but we'd always be stumped regarding what "we" could do.

But when we meet with Project Walk's CEO and learn about the franchising, that is the moment Mummy and I know. This is our next step; this is what my mummy and I had been searching for.

So, on January 24, 2015—during one of the biggest snowstorms of the winter—Project Walk Boston opens its doors. It is, in many ways, my family's gift not only to me but to others who have gone through challenges like we have. A place where families and people who have had such loss can heal and not feel alone.

The head trainer at our newly opened franchise is a veteran and has served as an army medic. John is tough, and he is strong, and he knows just how to push me.

"You're a professional athlete, so I'm going to train you like one."

I thought my training for swimming was hard, but it is nothing compared to this. Five days a week, five to six hours a day, I'm tested and pushed beyond my limits like never before. John is not kidding when he promises to train me like a professional athlete. John quickly learns how I operate and what makes me tick, and we both decide something very important and familiar . . .

Getting back on my feet is my next "gold medal."

The next "impossible" to make "possible."

"Are you in?"

"Yes. I want this more than anything."

"All right, let's get to work."

And so it begins . . .

Relentlessly pursuing the impossible and looking every day for any sign of life in my legs is, at times, incredibly frustrating. Day in and day out, nothing—not even a twitch. I witness other clients of Project Walk seeing their muscles twitch, and mine show *zero* life. Finding the motivation to keep going is a full-time job. Looking past the odds and past the lack of life in my legs is challenging. Having a trainer like John—who knows how to channel that frustration—is key.

Keep going.

Don't stop.

Never. Stop.

"Did you stop when you were fighting for your life?"

No.

"What about when you were training for London and when you won gold?"

No.

"So, why stop now?"

· · ·

Finding the motivation to keep going was at times a feat in and of itself.

Keep going.

Don't stop.

We athletes like to see results, normally right away. But anyone who truly has trained knows the frustration and that almost always the improvements are subtle and barely noticeable. But you know to stay the course no matter how hard and frustrating it is. But to achieve the "impossible" you must train as if NOTHING is impossible.

Again.

Again.

Again.

Over and over, pushing, moving, and praying that something will give. But doubt always seems to make its way in.

This has never been done before.

Am I crazy?

Is this really possible?

November 11, 2015. One twitch in my right leg, the first controlled muscle reaction in nearly ten years. That is all I need. That is the momentum.

As on the rest of the journey, it is the small victories that lead to the biggest achievements. This small and subtle twitch creates a momentum. And athletes love momentum.

You have one good game, one fast race, and that creates a confidence and drive unlike any other. You keep showing up because you see the progress you've made. You like the feeling of achievement and improvement. And you *never* stop there.

That twitch turns into an active quad muscle firing, which leads to a step, then another, and another. In March 2016, nearly ten years since becoming paralyzed, I am back on my feet as if nothing had ever been wrong. A step turned into a stair. That stair turned into a 27-inch box jump.

Of course, I couldn't stop there: jumping (still can't land though), biking, running, and a year almost to the day of returning to my feet, skiing in the Swiss Alps, each day continuing to defy the odds and continuing to train like I'd never trained before. Why did I train so hard? Because I know what it's like to lose it all, I know what it's like to fall down, and I'm *never* going back there and I'm *never* going to back down.

Never stop getting stronger and better.

Keep moving forward.

But like any major victory and any moment where you've "made it," it's come at a price. Blood, sweat, and tears go into every victory—big and small—and every "golden" moment. The second you raise the trophy or they put that medal around your neck and the anthem plays, you know it's come at a price. Challenges occur, and sometimes you fall to depths that you never knew possible. But then with every fall, you have the chance to rise higher than ever and be better than you were before.

The question is: Will you rise?

Every difficulty, every challenge, every tear, it's worth it.

Trust me.

Just go for it.

Be a living example of what *is* possible.

In our most difficult moments, we have two choices: we can cry, or we can try.

It's easy to get frustrated and cry—we're human and we all struggle with that. Crying releases emotion, and that, in turn, sometimes makes you feel better. It's cathartic and healing. So, some crying is okay—even good.

But it's not okay to keep crying and stop trying. I think of it like a gladiator who has been wounded in the battle. He's hurting, but he still stands and tries to put one foot in front of the other. I was wounded like that gladiator, but I am trying to stand and put one foot in front of the other. With tears and sweat, hope and optimism, I am amazed at what my body is capable of.

Don't stop.

Keep training.

Because in truth, I'll have to train each and every day for the rest of my life. Every day, I have to "trick" my body and remind it that it is *not* paralyzed. And if I don't train or if I get tired, my legs don't function as well, and my muscles don't fire as quickly. My neurological system is constantly trying to repair itself. When I encounter any type of stressor or sickness, the function in my legs is the first to go. There are days, in fact, when my legs simply don't work, and I just have to work a little harder to get them to function properly. I have never publicly spoken about that.

The nerve damage will never go away, and I still cannot feel my legs. I've worked hard to hide my injury, but no matter how far I run, I'll never be able to run away from the damage that was done all those years ago—and that's okay.

Initially though, this is a tough pill to swallow—especially since that damage could have been avoided. But I choose not to go down the path of "what if," because if I do, bitterness and regret will poison me for the rest of my life.

I'd rather deal with nerve pain and damage and lack of feeling in my legs and feet than go back to a wheelchair or worse—a vegetative state.

Never stop getting stronger and better.

Keep moving forward.

And as much as I know what it's like to lose it all, I also know what it's like to gain it all back—plus more. Falling down has been a common theme in my journey, but so has standing back up—both literally and figuratively.

Fall down ten times, but I will stand up the eleventh time.

With each time you fall, you have the chance to stand tall.

I'm reminded of that price every day.

As amazing and wonderful as it was to win that medal, winning the gold is not my "golden" moment. Medals and trophies and accolades are incredible, but, ultimately, they are material things. They do not define who I am. What truly defines me—and all of us—is how we overcome our challenges and how we live our lives in spite of the obstacles that come our way. What's truly important is what we learn on the inside and how we grow from our experiences.

Even the gift of being able to walk again comes with its own set of challenges. I think most people would assume that when I start walking, everything is instantly happy and wonderful. But getting back on my feet is *terrifying!* At the beginning—when I am barely walking—I am afraid that I will no longer be capable of doing everything I could do before. Walking is challenging, painful, and exhausting and I cannot go anywhere fast initially. It is an arduous process between my hot pink crutches and various kinds of leg braces. And then, there is the issue of my personal identity. The public knew me for being in a wheelchair—they don't know the walking Victoria. Even *I* don't know the walking Victoria. Half of the time, I don't even recognize myself. At times, I'm still thinking I need to grab my wheelchair from my car. Just the mere fact that I can stand up from the couch or reach the top cabinet is shocking. It takes a long time to get used to being "tall." And then there are all the comments and questions—especially in light of how the IPC and the media have dragged me through the mud, accusing me of not being "disabled enough."

What will people say or think?

Will the media try to turn things around?

These worries may sound silly, but they are real concerns and thoughts that keep me up at night. I am grateful to be back on my feet, but I am terrified of stepping out into the public eye. My newfound ability to walk isn't something I can keep to myself, and I ultimately have to share the news with the world. That will mean being a "symbol of hope" for others who are in wheelchairs, have a disability, or have TM. Of course, I'm happy to share my hope with others, but there's this little thing called survivor's guilt.

How come I got my legs back when the majority of paralyzed people are not so blessed?

I am, of course, very grateful. But I am also plagued with survivor's guilt and other emotions—which is very similar to how I felt when I came out of my vegetative state. Overcoming odds is a great blessing, but it does come with survivor's guilt. When you are a "medical miracle," no one hands you a manual on how to cope and handle your miracle. Guilt is kind of like a summer thunderstorm—the sun shines all day and then—*boom*: thunder strikes.

So many people do not "wake up"—let alone learn to function and survive somewhat normally. And so many people *never* regain the ability to walk, and run, and more. I faced that reality far too many times before I got "my miracle" and, with God's help, was able to overcome it.

My job on ESPN is amazing. But being on television brings many pressures—it does for everyone in the public light. However, going from disabled to not disabled in front of an audience turned up the pressure a bit.

At the same time, my television career with ESPN is blossoming, so is my ability to stand and walk and truly seem like "nothing had ever happened." When I was still in my wheelchair, it was a reminder to myself and those around me that something bad and serious had happened. Almost every day, some complete stranger would ask, "What's wrong with you?"

And so a part of me wonders . . .

Was there something wrong with me?

Am I now "normal"?

And what, exactly, is "normal"?

• • •

My experience of learning how to walk is a lot like preparing for the Olympics. You train and train, and that's all you think about. Eat, sleep, train, repeat. Your training actually becomes a coping method for all the stress and pressure. Then one day, they put a gold medal around your neck. Or one day, you stand and walk.

I did it.

I'm free.

Wait . . .

I'm free . . .

Finally.

It takes a long time for the reality of my freedom to sink in. I know I'm free, but I don't know it—at least, I don't grasp it until almost a year to the day of when I first walked in March of 2016.

It happens on a sunny day on a chairlift in the middle of the Alps in Schladming, Austria. I am in town covering the 2017 Special Olympics World Games, and in between shoots (I am covering skiing and snowboarding), I decide to hit the slopes.

It is a picturesque day, and as I admire the impeccable views on my way to the top of the mountain, I look down at the skis on my feet and up at the sunny blue skies and the mountains around me. My heart is beating and I'm smiling.

That's when I know . . .

I lived.

I'm really back.

And . . .

Better than before.

I don't know why it hits me on this particular day, but I know that it is a turning point in my journey. Not only am I back on my feet literally and back on the slopes (I had been a skier since the age of three), but I am back in every possible way—and even better. I am finally at peace within my soul. There has been so much pain that I fought to hide and escape from. And for a while, I even tried to escape from God. But on that day, on the chairlift, it is just me and God. I'd had many days when it was just God and me, but this time everything is okay. Now that all my other emotions have settled, I am able to finally believe that I am free.

The shock has worn off, and like a caterpillar that has struggled to escape its cocoon, I am a butterfly, and—for the first time in ten years—I can finally fly.

Let's go, Victoria.

Time to fly.

Although sometimes, it takes a little bit for your wings to start working.

16

THE PROMISE

2017

If you give me another chance and give me back my life
and everything that has been taken away from me,
I promise you that I will live boldly
and use my voice to change the world.

This is the promise I made to God.

In a desperate plea during one of my darkest nights, I cried out to God—praying that He would hear me and let me out. I wanted to live, but not in this painful vegetative state; I wanted to live life in the world and be free. I made a promise, and I knew that if God chose to restore my life to me, I would have to keep my promise to Him.

After I had that eye-to-eye connection with my mummy and began to crawl back slowly to the world, I never forgot that promise. As time went on, I began to see God answering my exact prayer. Blinking turned to noises; noises turned to one word, two words, and complete sentences. Little by little, I began to emerge back into the world. As terrifying as it was, it was also exciting. For four years, the world had gone on without me, and now I was able to participate and live—finally.

To others, the stages of my recovery seemed quick, although for me they felt like forever. To cope, I began to live life in the fast lane. Recovering, learning, getting stronger, and being independent were all full-time jobs, but I needed to "make up for lost time" and "catch up" with everyone else. And over time, that became my focus—instead of the promise I had made to God. Brief, incredible moments would pass, and I would be reminded of my promise. I always knew that one day I would have to revisit the past.

It's time to go back . . .

Even at the beginning of my journey, I knew I was meant to share my story. Since I had made the promise to God, and since He chose to restore my voice and my life, I was determined to turn my mess into a message. But this has been no easy task.

When I think about the possibility of telling people what happened to me in a book, I honestly have no idea where to begin. The last decade has been a blur, and I am still trying to make sense of it all. Plus, there is the whole thing of needing confidence in order to write a book. We're not talking about an essay or a small write-up; we're talking a *book*, but not a book about sunshine and butterflies. I would have to describe intimate details about horrific ordeals that nearly killed me—things I have fought so hard to forget and things I have buried in the deepest layers of my soul never to be shared. I am terrified to revisit these events.

You can do it, Victoria.

You need to share your story.

A mutual friend introduces me to an author by the name of Dan Brown. Dan is an incredibly talented and accomplished writer. He encourages me to share my story, and he believes in me and my ability to write it. When someone like Dan tells you to write, you write. Dan becomes an incredible mentor and helps me navigate the crazy world of publishing.

Then it's Joel Osteen, who, like Dan, encourages me to share my story and my testimony. I am introduced to Joel by one of his lead pastors, Craig Johnson. He had heard about my story through my pastor, Anthony Milas, and wanted Joel to hear it, too. Joel has been a key part in this journey and helped my mum and me know God better.

Every Sunday, while I was still in my vegetative state, my mum would turn the TV channel to his sermons, and his messages always provided us with the courage and faith to keep fighting. In the summer of 2016 I'm invited to take the stage with Joel at

Lakewood Church and then again at the Detroit Tigers stadium at America's Night of Hope, which is a truly life-changing and incredible experience. Afterward, Joel introduces me to his colleague Shannon. Between Shannon, Dan, and Joel, I have quite the team of supporters encouraging me to share my story.

I am excited to get started and share *my* story once and for all. And I want to tell it without outside influences putting their own spin on it. Raw, real, and me. No holding back and no more sugarcoating. God didn't give me my voice and this platform to tell half the truth. What good would that do for the person out there who is suffering like I once did?

The only issue is:

It hurts more the second time around.

Now that you've read this book, you know that I suffered some pretty horrific things. And if you had any idea of my story before this book, you may have been surprised by what you have read. I didn't really want to share all the bad parts. To tell the truth, I was embarrassed by the fact that I was so helpless and such a victim of abuse and neglect. I wanted to keep it to myself, but as a public figure, that's really hard to do. I got by for several years with sugarcoating my story, but there was always a small, strong voice deep down that would say, "You need to share the truth." I tried to ignore that voice, and I thought, *No, no, I'm NEVER sharing that. Not happening.*

Yet here I am.

As I begin, I am quickly reminded of how bad this journey really has been. I had worked so hard at "numbing" and "forgetting" that once I really start to dive into the details, I feel as if I am drowning. But going all in for this book means jumping right into the good, the bad, and the horrific.

Welcome aboard to the SS *Almost-Quarter-Life Crisis*, part two. Quickly, I am plagued with nightmares, panic attacks, crying spells, severe anxiety, and depression. I thought I'd dealt with all my feelings back in 2014; I thought I'd mourned my losses and faced what had happened. That was just part one of my almost-quarter-life crisis. That time was nothing compared to my writing experience. The year 2014 felt like a light summer shower, and writing this book feels like a massive hurricane.

You see, my body was and is strong and knew how to fight the physical trials and the abuse, but my heart and my brain and my emotions were a different story.

As I write, I am trying to stay afloat and do my job. Putting on a smile, traveling the world, and portraying this "perfect" life and career is not easy. At one of the highest points of my life I was also at one of the lowest. To the outside world I "had it all," was jet-setting around the world and living "the life" that so many people only dream of. In fact, a lot of my success has come out of the fear of going backwards. I am a very driven person, always have been. But this drive went into warp speed after I got sick.

Don't get me wrong: I am incredibly grateful for all that I have, but I am completely broken on the inside. And nobody knows, except for my mummy and grandma.

I even begin questioning why I survived, because living through it again is at times unbearable. There are a few moments in which I don't think I can keep going. There is even a moment before going on air that I am curled up in the fetal position on the phone with my mummy asking her to "remind me why I have to keep going, tell me that I have to live." Definitely not one of my proudest moments, but I have to keep it real.

• • •

Nightmares, panic attacks, crying spells, suicidal thoughts, immense pain, and crippling anxiety become daily occurrences for me as I dive into the scariest and darkest, most painful parts of my life and this journey.

PTSD and anxiety are very real and debilitating illnesses that try to break me down even when I think I am okay. At the end of the day: I was a child. A young, innocent child who had been kicked down over and over again. What should have been a treatable condition turned into a decade-long battle and a life-altering ordeal. What happened to me and what was done to me was devastating. And only those closest to me know the scars left behind from the abuse.

But I'm not bitter or angry—those are actually the two emotions I experience the least. Instead, when writing this book, I am heartbroken for that little girl who just wanted to go to field hockey camp and desperately wanted to fight and survive. Little Victoria simply wanted to be alive. She didn't want attention, and she didn't want to get sick. She just wanted to live the life she loved. And there are other Victorias out there. Maybe not exactly like me, but life is not easy for anyone.

I write this book and tell the truth for that little girl, me—the little girl whose innocence was violently ripped away. The little girl who had to lie alone, dying and trying to say good-bye to the ones she loved and telling herself it was "okay to let go." No child should ever have to do that, especially not alone. I'm still heartbroken for the girl whose first words after coming out of a vegetative state were "they hurt me." That's the first thing I said to my family. I think of that daily . . . although little by little, it hurts less.

In movies, we see these warriors using huge daggers and swords to literally pierce through their enemies. Daggers and swords are meant to kill you slowly. Inch by inch creating an unbearable pain that tortures the victim. Every move you make and every breath you take, the dagger's pain is felt even more. Only by lying still does the dagger become less painful, but when you stay still, you stop living.

Don't stop living.

Sometimes daggers are not physical but emotional. These emotional daggers are felt just as deeply.

Ouch.

I've been pierced by many daggers in my journey, but I kept

fighting with each piercing. I refused to pull out each dagger because I was afraid I'd bleed. I thought once I started bleeding it wouldn't stop and I'd bleed out.

For more than a decade I have lived with the emotional daggers of this journey. Without realizing it, I got used to the pain and the slow, steady piercing. I did my best to numb the pain and to forget I'd been stabbed. Then another dagger would pierce me . . . but I had to keep moving forward, no matter what.

More recently, though, I've started to acknowledge the daggers and the pain they cause. I picture them as rusty and old and sharp. It bothers me that they became such a norm in my life. They did not belong in me, but I had gotten so used to them that I didn't know or remember what it was like to not have them.

My daggers reveal themselves as I write. I relive years of pain and suffering. I begin to understand that I have to get them out. They have been holding me back. Just think about it for a moment: If you had a dagger—or two or ten—sticking out of your chest, it would be painful and would literally get in the way of everything.

It's easy to understand when it is a physical thing that you can see. But the invisible daggers are the deadly ones. You don't see how your everyday life can be affected. I began to relive a life of pain and suffering.

Bleed it out.

As each word, memory, and piece of this journey hits the paper, the daggers begin to be pulled out slowly. And I begin to bleed for the first time in well over a decade. At times the pain of these memories is unbearable. I gasp for air and try to face each and every terrifying moment in order to heal. But once again—thanks to my *Grey's Anatomy* medical knowledge—I understand that only when I allow myself to bleed do my wounds begin to heal.

I have a promise to fulfill, and sometimes keeping our promises is not easy. God has answered my prayer and has given me a life— one even better than I could imagine. Sometimes what we want to do and what we have to do is not easy. The easy way out is pain free for the most part, and the hard way almost always involves some kind of pain.

Don't forget the promise.

After I looked death straight in the eye, I also looked at life with a far more grateful and determined heart. Achieving all that I have at twenty-three and continuing to climb, in many ways, has been my own way of proving that I am alive. Most people see the sunshine but didn't know the storm that took place before the sun came out. To have watched the world go on without me for so many years trapped in a hospital bed created an invisible hamster wheel that I was continually running on. Even if I was tired . . . I kept running.

Never stop running.

Every day we each have our struggles and battles. It's easy to run away and hide, but they'll eventually catch up to you. Eventually, you'll have to sit down and watch and live and feel. It's not fun and can be insanely painful yet also at the same time incredibly powerful. You can take back control of your inner peace and fight those memories and painful moments that have worked so hard to pull you down. You just have to have faith and the fight. I learned a lot about fighting over the years, but six months of writing taught me more about fighting than the past eleven years.

As I've said over this entire journey, I would never choose what happened to me—but I would never change it. Who I've become and where my life is going and where I've come from are all far beyond my wildest dreams. I would like to have not suffered so much. But then again, extraordinary challenges and pain can lead to extraordinary experiences and an extraordinary life.

• • •

Throughout this journey I have battled an external force. The best way to describe it is when you're underwater and you let all the air out of your body, and you begin to sink. I'm a swimmer, and the water has always been my special place. But for the last decade I have been fighting to reach the surface. Each time I got close, something would happen to pull me back down—whether it was getting sick, the IPC drama, the fear of death and the unknown or, even more recently, facing and coming to terms with what happened to me.

There have been times I've been tempted to stop swimming and give in to the force that was pulling me underwater.

Life at times can be confusing and hard and frustrating. Unbeknownst to most of us, we are fighting a force that wants to pull us under. But each time you have a decision to make: sink or swim. Each wave hits and sometimes it knocks the wind out of you. Other times the water is calm and serene, and you can peacefully drift and marvel at the wonder of it all.

Just keep swimming.

Even when it hurts.

Even when you can't keep going . . .

Keep going.

Swimming to the surface when it feels like you're sinking is easier said than done. But it took that moment on the chairlift in Austria to realize that. It's okay sometimes to sink a little bit. You just have to keep yourself from getting too far down. Keep moving even if it's not as strongly as you'd like it to be.

Just keep swimming.

Swimming is a sport of constant movement. Whether it's the Olympics or the lake or swimming to stay alive, they all have the same theme: constant movement. The minute you stop moving is when you sink or lose, drown, or drift away. Life, at least in my experience, is like a constant swim. Sometimes the waters are calm and serene and picturesque, and other times they are choppy and uncertain and dangerous. But if we stop moving, we don't move forward. And life is all about moving forward. Never allowing the waters of life to get stagnant or dry out. Keep turning even if you do not know where you are swimming to sometimes. That is okay. After all, we really have to take the swim one stroke at a time. Day by day, moment by moment. Sometimes it's hard to swim and that is okay.

You'll get there.

I promise.

When it feels like you'll never reach the surface, keep going. When the waters seem too deep, never lose sight of the light above the surface. That light is bright, and it is yours regardless of how far you've sunk down or how tired you are.

Take back that light.

Reach the surface.

I've learned over and over and over again that when you feel like stopping and when you feel like giving up—*that* is the time when you have to find everything you have to keep going.

But sometimes you've battled the rough waters and you reach the surface, only to find that there are cliffs and mountains ahead of you.

What do you do?

Do you give up?

Give in?

Or climb?

It's scary to climb and take that leap, especially after battling rough waters. You're tired and weak. You're running on empty and you feel as if you've got nothing left. No more fight. But that is the moment when you find it within you to climb. Mountains can be daunting and scary and at times "impossible" to climb. But think about the photos you've seen and maybe even the views you've experienced.

Some of the toughest climbs have the prettiest views.

This mountain I have been climbing for over ten years at times felt endless. It felt like I was never going to make it to the top. But my promise to God was to live boldly and use my voice to change the world. And that's just what I planned to do. When climbing a mountain, there are moments when it seems impossible and when it is beyond challenging and painful. But if you keep climbing despite the obstacles, you WILL make it to the top and maybe even have a victory dance.

17

VICTORY DANCE

September 18, 2017

"Dancing the cha-cha, Victoria Arlen with her partner Val Chmerkovskiy."

That's me.

Holy moly.

This is it, standing on the *Dancing with the Stars* dance floor as one of the celebrities chosen for Season 25 in hot pink, sparkly, fringy pants and a bedazzled crop top. Looking out and around at the place I dreamed of as a little girl. I even had this dream during some of my most painful moments, watching from a hospital bed in the ICU or the hospital bed in my living room. I am here, in the game, not on the sidelines anymore and paired with by far the best teammate, Mr. Valentin Chmerkovskiy.

Before every dance, there is an intro montage that plays for audiences at home and in the ballroom. The video for week one introduces each celebrity and tells their story of making it to *Dancing with the Stars*. As you can imagine, mine is a tearjerker. I have never publicly shared a lot of what is played in the video—in particular the incredibly heartbreaking footage of me fighting for my life. I would consider myself pretty immune to everything I went through. Especially after the year of emotional healing that had taken place. But this moment in particular is unlike anything I had ever experienced.

Watching the video before my dance, I see that little girl fighting for her life in a hospital bed. The footage is heartbreaking, and for the first time, I feel that pain so strongly I want so badly to reach out to little Victoria and tell her to hold on and keep fighting. That everything was going to be all right. In an instant, I snap right back to that place of pain and am nearly paralyzed. I feel my chest tighten, my hands shake, and tears start to well up in my eyes.

How could this be?

How did I get here?

I was paralyzed a year and a half ago, and now I'm about to dance in front of millions.

I can't even feel my legs.

I don't even know which foot I'm using.

This seems impossible.

Is this really happening?

For a split second, I feel locked in and trapped by these thoughts and emotions that flood my brain like a tsunami. But then I hear an excited voice yell, "Victoria, Victoria, look at me." I look up at Val, who is smiling from ear to ear. "This is *your* time." In that moment I immediately snap back to the beautiful and wonderful reality. I am alive, on my two feet about to dance a cha-cha and show the world that nothing is impossible. I knew from the first day of rehearsals this was for a far greater purpose.

Click.

Click.

Click.

Click.

The four clicks start (which is the audible intro beat that happens before every dance) and all I can do is look up and thank God. My heart overflows with gratitude. As the music begins, my gaze turns to the camera and then to my partner, Val, who excitedly proclaims, as he runs over and grabs my hand, "Let's go change the world!" And in an instant (one minute and eleven seconds to be exact), we do just that. As we dance, we prove to millions that despite insurmountable odds and challenge after challenge, you can be victorious.

This is by far one of the most powerful and memorable moments of my life. Far beyond anything I could have ever imagined. I realize I am not that little girl in the hospital bed. I am alive, free, in pink, sparkly, fringy pants and DANCING on *Dancing with the Stars.* The very show that at ten years old I proudly proclaimed to my mummy that I would be a part of one day. And when I was sick, my parents would turn on the show hoping I was "in there" and still dreaming and believing. The show that at many times was my escape from the horrific and painful moments of this journey.

In an instant, this whole journey has come full circle. As the music ends and the pyrotechnics commence, I can't stop smiling. And for the first time in a long time, I am speechless. "You did it, I'm so proud of you! Tonight, you changed the world," Val says as we tearfully embrace each other and celebrate. I'm honestly speechless. This moment is bigger than the both of us realized and so much more than just a dance. I can't help but feel this insane amount of gratitude for the second chance at life that I was given. And to see my parents in the crowd crying tears of joy, all I can think is . . .

I'm really glad I lived.

As the crowd roars and Tom Bergeron walks over with a huge smile and proudly says, "Look at what you just did," I also realize another significant thing.

I made it to the top of the mountain, and this is my victory dance.

All those years of pain and suffering and fighting have turned to joy, gratitude, and dancing. For those who truly know me, I LOVE to dance. This is that moment where I clearly see firsthand the purpose for all that I had gone through.

Purpose for the pain.

Dancing with the Stars, aside from all of the glitz and glamour, is one of the biggest healing experiences for me. It is actually healing that I didn't even realize I needed.

Before I left for *Dancing with the Stars*, I had been crippled with severe post-traumatic stress from this journey. It took ten years for it all to hit me. Only a handful of those closest to me knew what I was going through. They knew the unbearable pain I was in. But nobody else knew. I know how to put my warrior face on and oftentimes I hid behind my smile. I still struggled with finding a purpose for everything I had gone through. I had brief moments when I could start to understand, but for the most part, it didn't make any sense until that first dance on September 18, 2017.

Throughout this journey, God has sent people along the way who have helped me heal. Like a puzzle, each person represented a piece coming together to help me be whole again. It's kind of like when I was little and would dump out all the pieces on the floor and then, one by one, connecting the pieces I could see the picture as a whole. But in the beginning, it was a mess.

I was a puzzle.

And I was a mess.

At this point in my journey most of the pieces of the puzzle are together. But there are still a few missing . . .

Each dance has a message and a story to tell, and in each dance, Val teaches me how to hold my head up and fly. He pushes me like

Coach John pushed me in the pool and like John pushed me at Project Walk. He doesn't see what I can't do and instead empowers me with what I can do.

Holy crap!

Despite me not being able to feel my legs, Val teaches me how to DANCE, something I never in a million years imagined myself doing again. It was actually one of the things I missed the most when I was so sick. I'd spend hours imagining dancing again, and now here I am—dancing. We found a system and a way of helping my legs and me connect. Val and I would often come up with key words. While viewers watched in delight on the TV and heard the beautiful music, Val and I would be yelling words like, "bunny, shrimp, left, puppy, right, your favorite, zigzag, point, take off, glide, quick quick slow, and down" . . . to name a few. Week after week I continue to improve and be pushed by Val. And *intense* is an understatement: five plus hours a day in the studio and countless hours after rehearsals envisioning and making sure my legs would keep working. Spasms were still pretty evident, but believe it or not, when I started dancing, my spasms got better, the nerve pain in my back got better, and I was even able to walk better. In every possible way, dance was the final piece of healing after this long and painful journey. It allowed me to be free in every way and truly see what my body was capable of. But learning to dance was ten times harder than learning to walk.

Seriously.

But every day, each time I set foot on the dance floor, I am reminded of what I can do, and I find a greater purpose for all the pain I have endured. We are changing lives. Each step and each time we dance, a small piece of me is put back together and my eyes twinkle a little brighter. My family sees it, I see it, and the world sees it. I am constantly reminded that nothing is impossible. *I'm* possible. The mere fact that I am dancing is a miracle itself. But beyond that, I learn how to hold my head up, something I haven't been able to do in well over a decade.

Aside from teaching me to dance each week, Val pushes me to stand tall and confident and proud. Which is something I never really embraced. For years, I had been knocked down, and so, over time I got used to having my head down. Being in a wheelchair and being stared at and looked down upon by my peers for years caused me to go into my cocoon. I was told well over a hundred times and even as I began to walk, I still would keep my head down for different reasons. Mainly for the fear of falling over and also to see which foot was stepping first. Not feeling my legs made it really difficult to maneuver when I was walking. But I just got used to having my head down. I didn't realize it, but this journey had taken its toll and left me with a heavy heart and my head down. Aside from the accomplishments and blessings, there was so much that I held in. But like all habits, good or bad, over time we get used to them. I got used to keeping my head down and being in a cocoon. But I was never meant to stay there, and God definitely had another plan for me.

I was meant to fly.

And . . .

Dancing with the Stars *is my flying lesson . . .*

• • •

Hold your head up.

It's your time to shine.

• • •

The people I meet and the lifelong friends I make on the show are simply the icing on the cake of an incredible experience. They, too, play an immense role in helping me stand tall and shine. On top of all the amazing things, another part of me healed. For years since I returned to the world, birthdays were always incredibly tough for me. On my fifteenth birthday in 2009, I really did not think I'd make it to see another birthday. As much as Father Bashobora was providing hope, in my heart I thought that my time was up. I said good-bye to my family and, more important, I held on to sharing one final birthday with my brothers. Since then birthdays always held a heavy place in my heart. That was until my twenty-third birthday, when not only did I share it with my incredible *Dancing with the Stars* family, who surprised me with a cake and tiara, I got to share it with the millions of viewers, forever changing my views on birthdays and giving me a memory that made all the ones in the past disappear like the frosting on cake. (Fun fact: I LOVE frosting!) Finally, I am no longer watching from the sidelines. I am in the game with the best possible team.

You did it.

We did it.

This is the mountaintop and that view I had been dreaming about. And it is even better than I could ever imagine. And a reminder that some of the tougher climbs have the most beautiful views.

• • •

Facing our fears allows us to *embrace* our fears, which allows us to *defy* our fears and eventually *conquer* our fears.

Face it, embrace it, defy it, conquer it.™

Find the courage, feel the fear, take the pain, and keep going. It gets better. I promise. Keep climbing, even when it hurts. I promise you . . . the view is worth it, and the victory dance is better than you could ever imagine.

The best is yet to come.

And . . .

I'm just getting started.

SPECIAL THANKS

As I reflect on who I need to thank from my tragic, beautiful journey, I am reminded of the moment when I realized that not only can I not write about every detail of this journey, but I can't possibly write about every amazing angel. If I had tried, my book would have surely been more than one thousand pages long. The angels who came in and out of my life these last twelve years all had a reason and a season. You all know who you are, and take solace in knowing you have a very special place in my heart. Thank you, thank you, thank you . . . you have all been the wind beneath my wings and for that I am eternally grateful. I love you all. Thank you for giving me the wings to fly.